DO-IT-YOURSELF

Wills, Power of Attorney & Probate

Wills, Power of Attorney & Probate

The contents of this Guide have been approved under Scottish law by Neill Clerk & Murray, Solicitors.

© 2003 Law Pack Publishing Limited
Reprinted 2004

Law Pack Publishing Limited
76-89 Alscot Road
London SE1 3AW

www.lawpack.co.uk

Printed in Great Britain

ISBN: 1 904053 33 5

Important facts

This book contains the information and instructions necessary to make your own Will, create an Enduring or Continuing Power of Attorney, a General or Welfare Power of Attorney, a Living Will and obtain a grant of probate or letters of administration, and administer an estate, without a solicitor. This Guide is for use in England and Wales, and Scotland but is not suitable for use in Northern Ireland. The law is stated as at 1st August 2003.

The information it contains has been carefully compiled from professional sources, but its accuracy is not guaranteed, as laws and regulations may change or be subject to differing interpretations.

Neither this nor any other publication can take the place of a solicitor on important legal matters. As with any legal matter, common sense should determine whether you need the assistance of a solicitor rather than rely solely on the information and forms in this book.

We strongly urge you to consult a solicitor if:

- substantial amounts of money are involved;

- you do not understand the instructions;

- what you want to do is not precisely covered by this book.

Table of contents

Part 3: Probate

How to use this book

Wills, Powers of Attorney & Probate can help you achieve important legal objectives conveniently, efficiently and economically. Remember that it is important for you to use this book properly if you are to avoid later difficulties.

Step-by-step instructions

1. Read this guide carefully. If after thorough examination you decide that your requirements are not met by this book, or you do not feel confident about writing your own documents, consult a solicitor.

2. This guide refers to Law Pack Will Forms and other legal forms and documents. You can obtain original documents from the sources referred to on page 153; examples are included for reference when preparing you own.

3. When completing your own forms, do not leave any section blank, unless instructed otherwise. If any section is inapplicable, write 'not applicable', 'none' or 'nil' to show you have not overlooked the section. You should also make copies of the completed forms.

4. Always use a pen or type on legal documents; never use pencil.

5. Do not cross out or erase anything you have written on your final forms.

6. You will find a helpful glossary of terms at the end of this book. Refer to this glossary if you find unfamiliar terms.

7. Always keep legal documents in a safe place and in a location known to your spouse, family or solicitor.

Introduction

It is so off-putting that most people keep putting it off - making a Will that is. Seven out of ten of us have never got around to it and half of us never will; this can lead to problems for your loved ones, as the rules of intestacy determine who get what.

Making a Will can be a simple do-it-yourself action that makes family and friends lives much easier - and it ensures they get what you want. It can be inexpensive, only a matter of filling in a specially prepared document with the help of easy-to-read instructions and information that ensure your last wishes do come true.

Asking somebody to do something for you is an everyday matter: you ask a friend to pick up your dry cleaning or post your letters. But if you want someone to act on your behalf on more weighty matters with full legal authority, so they can buy and sell your shares for example, the law requires and provides a means for doing this: a 'power of attorney'.

If the power of attorney is to be on a long-term basis complications arise in the event of the person giving the power becoming mentally 'incapacitated'. This could happen either because of old age or serious illness. And as medical knowledge and life expectancy advance it is becoming more and more important to plan for a time when you may not be able to make decisions for yourself. This Guide tells you how you can most effectively protect your assets should you become unable to communicate your wishes in the future, by creating an 'enduring' power of attorney (or 'continuing' power of attorney in Scotland).

Most people would admit to knowing little about how probate (called Confirmation in Scotland) – the procedure of taking out a 'grant of probate' and subsequent administration of an estate – works. One's first encounter with it is usually after the death of a loved one.

More often than not people are taken by surprise when told they have been named an executor – or 'executrix' if female – in a deceased's Will. The executor may have no knowledge of the deceased's wishes or the whereabouts, let alone the contents, of the Will and other important documents. The funeral and disposal of the testator's remains may have to be carried out without reference to their wishes simply because the Will has not been found. Sometimes those who have been named executors are unable to fulfil their duties and a beneficiary of the estate may need to act as administrator of the estate. When these complications, along with all the other responsibilities that must be attended to following a death, come to light during the mourning period, it becomes clear why it is best to be well prepared for executorship.

This Guide aims to prepare you for all the above responsibilities.

Part 1

Last Will & Testament

Chapter 1:
Everyone needs a Will

Without a valid Will you cannot control who will inherit your property after your death. Should you die intestate (without a Will), your property will be distributed according to law, which may well be inconsistent with your personal wishes. In some cases, where you have no traceable relatives, your estate may go to the Crown instead of the people you want to benefit.

By making a Will you can determine precisely who will inherit your property and let your loved ones know that you have considered their needs.

Equally important, you can determine who will administer your estate and who will act as guardian for your minor children if they are left without a surviving parent. A Will can also express your preferences for burial or cremation and for donating organs or your body for medical purposes. In addition, making a Will gives you the opportunity to reduce your inheritance tax liability. This is particularly important if you have substantial assets.

If you die leaving a valid Will that appoints one or two executors who are still living at the time of your death, legal ownership of all of your property passes automatically to those executors. They must apply to the Probate Registry (a division of the civil court) in England and Wales or to the Commissary Office of the appropriate Sheriff Court in Scotland for a legal document confirming their right to administer your property and to distribute it to your beneficiaries. This application process is called 'obtaining probate' or in Scotland, 'obtaining Confirmation'.

Who should make a Will?

Every adult can and should make a Will. The only qualification necessary is that you be of legal age, which is 18 in England and Wales and 12 in Scotland. Any member of active military service in time of war who is over 14 and desires to make a Will is excepted from the age requirement. Underage seamen at sea during peacetime also may make a valid Will.

You must also be of sound mind. 'Sound mind' means you understand what you are giving away, how you are giving it away, and to whom you are giving it. If you have a history of mental disorder or if an illness may be affecting your judgment in any way, consult a qualified doctor before preparing your Will. This helps establish your competence and will be useful should your Will be contested later on the grounds of mental incapacity.

If you are married, you and your spouse should both prepare Wills even if marital assets are primarily in the name of one spouse. Usually you name your spouse as your main beneficiary and include a 'substitutional beneficiary' (see chapter 8) to take effect if your spouse predeceases you.

It is particularly important to make a Will if you are not married but are living with someone whom you want to benefit from your estate. Because the rules of intestacy make no provision for unmarried partners, if you die intestate your partner would receive nothing from your estate.

English or Scottish property left in a foreign Will is governed by English or Scots law respectively. An English or Scottish Will dealing with land in a foreign country will normally be governed, for the purposes of distribution, by the laws of the country where the land is located.

Dying intestate

If you die without making a Will, or if your Will is invalid, you die intestate. The management of your estate, which is your house (if any) and other assets minus your debts and liabilities, is then placed in the hands of administrators (called executors-dative in Scotland) appointed by the court, who are likely to be close members of your family.

In England and Wales, the administrators distribute your estate according to the rules of intestacy established by the Administration of Estates Act 1925; these apply to anyone whose domicile or permanent home at the time of death is England or Wales, or in some cases to one whose home is abroad but who retains English domicile.

In Scotland, the rules of intestacy, established by the Succession (Scotland) Act 1964 as amended, apply to anyone whose domicile or permanent home at the time of death is Scotland or in some cases to one whose home is abroad but who retains Scottish domicile.

In effect, these rules allow your surviving spouse and dependants to claim your property and money without regard to your wishes. If no surviving relatives can be found, your entire estate goes to the Crown.

The rules of intestacy in England and Wales

The rules of intestacy are complex. The effect of the rules depends partly on the size of your estate. If your estate is large, less than you expect may go to your spouse. Broadly speaking, funeral expenses and administration costs are deducted from your estate. The remaining property is distributed as follows:

1.   If only your spouse survives you, he or she receives all of the property remaining in your estate, provided that he or she survives for 28 days after your death.

2.   If your spouse survives you by 28 days and you are also survived by children

   a.   your surviving spouse receives:

      (i)   a 'statutory legacy' of up to £125,000 plus the interest accrued from the time of death until payment. The statutory legacy is free from tax and costs.

      (ii)   all household and personal items of the deceased ('personal chattels').

      (iii)   a trust (called a 'life estate') consisting of half of the estate after the initial £125,000 and the personal chattels have been deducted. The spouse is said to have a 'life interest'; that is, he or she is entitled to receive income for life from this trust, but may not spend the capital.

   b.   the children receive:

      (i)   half of the remaining estate divided equally among them.

      (ii)   the right to inherit, upon the death of the surviving spouse, the half of the estate in which that spouse had a life estate. This life estate is divided equally among the surviving children. If any of your children have predeceased you leaving their own child/children, their child/children will automatically take their parent's share by substitution.

3.   If your spouse survives you by 28 days and, instead of children, there are parents, brothers, sisters, nieces and/or nephews

   a.   your surviving spouse receives:

      (i)   up to £200,000 plus the interest accrued from the time of death until payment.

      (ii)   all household and personal items of the deceased.

(iii) absolute title to half of the estate after the initial £200,000 and the personal chattels have been deducted.

b. your surviving parents receive absolute title to the other half of the estate, to be divided equally between them.

c. if there are no surviving parents, the other half of your estate is inherited absolutely by brothers and sisters of the whole blood equally, or their children equally. If there is none the entire estate, however large, goes to your spouse.

4. If there is no surviving spouse but there are surviving children, your estate is divided equally among the children. If any of your children have predeceased you leaving their own child/children, their child/children will automatically take their parent's share by substitution.

a. They inherit immediately if they have achieved the age of 18 or are married.

b. Your estate is held in trust for minor children until they reach the age of 18 or marry.

5. If there is no surviving spouse or children but you are survived by your parents, they receive absolute title to your entire estate to be divided equally between them.

6. If there is no surviving spouse, children or parents, your estate is inherited in the following order:

a. brothers and sisters equally, or their children equally, if none

b. half-brothers and half-sisters equally, or their children equally, if none

c. grandparent(s) equally, if none

d. uncles and aunts of whole blood equally, or their children equally, if none

e. uncles and aunts of half blood equally, or their children equally, if none

f. the Crown.

The money your surviving spouse receives from your estate under a life interest is placed in trust. Whilst the right to receive interest from this trust is for life, that interest is not likely to be enough to live on. Remember, the capital must remain intact and cannot be touched by your surviving spouse. Upon his or her death, the capital passes on to whoever inherited the other half.

The rules of intestacy in Scotland

The following rules of distribution apply to all property that is not dealt with by a valid Will.

1. All debits and funeral expenses and all and any liability for inheritance tax are paid out of your estate.

2. If your spouse survives then he or she will be entitled to 'prior rights' comprising:

    a. a dwellinghouse (subject to any burdens affecting it) in which the spouse was ordinarily resident at the date of your death up to the value of £130,000 (current figure) (or cash of £130,000 if the dwellinghouse has a greater value than £130,000);

    b. furniture and plenishings up to the value of £22,000 (current figure);

    c. a financial right: if you leave issue the amount of £35,000 and if you leave no issue the amount of £58,000 (current figures).

    After payment of prior rights the rest of your estate is referred to as the 'residue'.

3. If your spouse and issue survive, the residue is divided in the following manner:

    a. one-third to your spouse; and

    b. two-thirds to your issue (your children and the issue of predeceasing children).

4. If you leave no issue, the residue is divided as follows:

    a. one-half to your spouse (or whole if no one survives under (b)); and

    b. one-half (or whole if your spouse does not survive) between:

        (i)   to extent of one-half (or whole if no one survives under (ii)) to brothers and sisters (and issue of predeceasing brothers and sisters); and

        (ii) to extent of remaining half (or whole if no one survives under (i)) to parents.

5. If no one survives to take as in 4., then the residue is divisible among maternal and paternal uncles and aunts (and issue of predeceasing uncles and aunts).

6. If no one survives to take as in 5., then the residue will go to paternal and maternal grandparents and if either paternal or maternal grandparents shall not survive then to the brothers and sisters of such paternal or maternal grandparents (and issue of such brothers and sisters of paternal or maternal grandparents).

7. If no one survives to take as in 6., then it will go to the Crown as the ultimate heir (known in legal terms as the *ultimus haeres*).

A mistress, common-law wife, spouse separated by judicial decree and a divorced spouse have no right to inherit under the laws of intestacy. In England and Wales, a spouse separated by an order from the Magistrates' Court does retain the right to benefit under the laws of intestacy.

It is also possible to die partially intestate. This occurs if you fail to deal with all of your property in your Will, or if a beneficiary dies before you and you have not provided for that contingency. If any part of the inheritance cannot be given to another beneficiary named under the Will, that part must be distributed according to the laws of intestacy.

As you can see, dying without a Will robs you of the right to decide who will inherit your estate. You will avoid intestacy if you make a valid Will in accordance with the instructions in this book.

Chapter 2:
How long is a Will valid?

Once prepared, your Will is valid until revoked, which may occur in a number of ways:

1. **By destruction**, combined with your intention to revoke. Destroying a Will can be achieved by intentionally burning, tearing or otherwise destroying it. Accidental destruction of a Will does not cancel it but there might be difficulty in establishing that it applies. A Will can be destroyed by another person, but it must be at the request of the testator.

    A Will must be physically destroyed; simply crossing out the Will or writing 'revoked' across may not be sufficient. Erasing or cutting off the signature of the testator or witnesses may be enough to revoke the Will.

    If part of a Will is destroyed, only that part of the Will is revoked. If an entire Will is to be revoked, any codicils attached to it may have to be revoked separately. If a Will is known to have been kept in your possession, yet is absent at your death and cannot be found, it will be presumed that it was intentionally destroyed by you unless there is contrary evidence of your intentions.

2. **By making a new Will** that revokes your old Will (but if not destroyed your old Will may be revived if the new Will is revoked). In order to do this, the Will forms in this book contain the phrase, 'I revoke all previous Wills and codicils'. This gives you the opportunity to reconsider all of the provisions of the old Will and make all the changes at one time rather than separately by way of codicils. Be sure your new Will complies with all the requirements necessary to make a valid Will.

3. **In England and Wales (but not in Scotland) by marriage or re-marriage**, unless your Will expressly states that it is made in contemplation of your forthcoming marriage. Your Will is automatically revoked by marriage unless these three conditions are met:

    *   You were planning to marry when your Will was made.

- Your Will names the specific person you married.

- You state that you want the Will to remain in effect during your marriage to that person.

Other than in one of the above circumstances, your Will remains valid for an unlimited period of time. Note that divorce does not automatically revoke a Will in England and Wales or in Scotland.

4. **In Scotland by the birth of a child** if the Will makes no provision for such child and revocation cannot be rebutted by evidence of intention.

When is a new Will necessary?

It is a good idea to review your Will from time to time, so that it is always up to date. But you may need to revise your Will at any time for a number of reasons. Common reasons for revising a Will include:

Changes in the family

When a baby is born, a child becomes 18 (or perhaps some significant later age) or there is a death, your Will should be reviewed.

Marriage

In England and Wales (but not in Scotland) marriage automatically revokes a previous Will unless your Will expressly states that it is made in contemplation of that forthcoming marriage.

Divorce

Unlike marriage in England and Wales, divorce does not revoke a previous Will. But in England and Wales (not in Scotland) if your former spouse is named as a beneficiary, upon divorce he or she ceases to be a beneficiary or to receive a gift unless your Will expressly provides that the gift should still take effect if you divorce. In England and Wales (but not in Scotland) if your former spouse was named executor, upon divorce he or she will no longer be allowed to act as executor or obtain probate of your Will. It is best to make a new Will whenever you get divorced.

Change in financial circumstances

Have you acquired assets that you would like to give to particular beneficiaries? Or perhaps in hard times your estate may have become insufficient to cover the gifts you have made. Rewrite your Will upon a change in financial circumstances.

Changes in taxation

If your estate is large enough to attract tax, new taxes, reliefs or changes in the rates may call for changes in your Will.

Living abroad

It is normally desirable to make a Will in the country where you reside. This simplifies the administration of your estate and may also be helpful if you need to establish a change of domicile. Seek local advice if you prepare a Will in a foreign country.

How to revise your Will

Never attempt to revise or change your Will by altering it. The way to revise an existing Will is to prepare a new Will containing a clause revoking all previous Wills. The completed examples of the Will Forms at the back of this book contain revocation clauses. For safety, however, you should also physically destroy any former Will so that it cannot be mistaken for your most recent Will. Make sure you destroy all copies of your former Will as well.

Remember, you should not add words or provisions, nor should you change, delete, cross out or erase any part of your Will once it has been prepared. Do not staple, clip or attach any other documents to your Will.

Chapter 3: Writing your Will

Some people's circumstances require advice beyond the scope of this book. Seek the advice of a solicitor when writing your Will if you have a particularly complex estate, if you require tax planning advice, or if any of the following situations apply to you:

- You have power of appointment under a trust.

- Your permanent domicile is not in England, Wales or Scotland.

- You own property not located in England, Wales or Scotland.

- You own a farm.

- You own your own business or are involved in a partnership.

- You are a shareholder in a private, family-owned company.

- You are involved in a Lloyd's underwriting syndicate.

- You are separated but not divorced from your spouse.

- You intend to omit your spouse or children from your Will.

- You wish to create a life interest or other trust for another person.

This list is by no means exhaustive. If you are in doubt, consult a solicitor.

Preparing to make your Will

Before you make your Will:

- List the assets you own

- Decide who is to receive those assets

Make an inventory of everything you own, including any death benefits from life policies and pension funds that you expect to receive, whether in your name alone or owned jointly with others.

Next, decide whether there are specific gifts you want to make to particular people. As we explain later, any item you do not specifically allocate forms part of the 'residue' of your estate. You must also decide who is to receive this residue.

If you decide not to leave anything (a) in England and Wales to dependants or close relatives; or (b) in Scotland to your spouse or children (or issue of predeceasing children), some risk of challenge may arise. When this risk occurs, you should always consult a solicitor to assist in drafting your Will.

In England and Wales, if they are not provided for in your Will, the following people have six months from the date of grant of probate or letters of administration to file a claim against your estate:

1. Your surviving spouse.

2. A former spouse who has not remarried.

3. Any children, regardless of age.

4. Any other person, for example a step-child, who, as a result of your marriage, you treated as a child of the family.

5. Anyone who, for the whole of the period of two years immediately before your death, was cohabiting with you as your husband or wife.

6. Anyone who was financially dependent upon you, either wholly or in part, immediately prior to your death.

Legal rights in Scotland

In Scotland, a surviving spouse and children (and issue of predeceasing children, but no one else) are entitled to the following claims as an alternative to but not in addition to any benefits provided for in your Will:

1. A surviving spouse may claim (*ius relictae* or *ius relicti*) one-third of your moveable estate (i.e. all of your estate other than the house, land and buildings) or one-half of your moveable estate if no issue survive.

2. Children (and issue of predeceasing children) may claim (*legitim*) one-third of your moveable estate, or one-half of your moveable estate if no spouse survives. Therefore if such claims are made your Will may only be able to deal with (a) your heritable estate (i.e. house, land and buildings); and (b) one-third (or one half if either only spouse or only issue survive) of your moveable estate (which is sometimes called 'the dead's part').

Witnesses to your Will

To ensure the validity of your Will, it is important to have it properly witnessed. In England and Wales you need two witnesses aged over 18. In Scotland only one independent witness aged over 16 is required. In England and Wales you should choose people who are likely to be available when your executors apply for a grant of probate, in case a question should arise concerning the validity of your Will. A blind person cannot witness a Will.

Warning: It is vital that the witnesses to your Will are not beneficiaries under the Will. If a beneficiary (or in England or Wales his or her spouse) does witness your Will, the beneficiary may lose the benefit of his or her gift, but the Will remains valid.

In England and Wales an executor can safely act as a witness unless he or she is also a beneficiary or the spouse of a beneficiary. (This is considered bad practice in Scotland.)

Signing your Will

You must sign your Will **on each page** in the presence of two witnesses (or one in Scotland), who must both sign **on the last page only below** (or alongside) your signature and in your presence. The witnesses, however, do not have to sign in each other's presence (although in England and Wales the standard attestation clause requires them to do this so it is better if they are both present), nor do they have to be acquainted with the contents of the Will (although in England and Wales they must know they are signing a Will).

It is important that the full names and addresses of the witnesses are added after their signatures (or included in a testing or attestation clause). All signatories should use their usual signatures and write in ink. The Will should then be clearly dated. In England and Wales if one of the witnesses is a foreigner, the other witness must guarantee that the person had a sufficient knowledge of English to understand or that the proceedings were translated into his or her native language.

Testing or attestation clause: This is the signature clause, and explains who signed the Will and the conditions under which it was signed. This clause in a properly executed Will ensures that the validity of the Will will not be questioned. It ensures compliance with the law of the execution of Wills. If this clause is absent from the Will, it may be necessary to have an affidavit, which is a sworn statement, from one of the witnesses when the Will goes to probate. This can be a problem if that witness is dead or cannot be located.

Chapter 4:
Executors and guardians

By taking the time to prepare a Will, you have the advantage of naming your executor(s). If you leave no Will and die intestate, the court appoints an administrator (in Scotland called an executor-dative) to take charge of your estate. If none of your relatives is willing to take the job, the court may appoint a stranger who, completely unaware of and not bound by your last wishes, distributes your property according to the rules of intestacy.

You should appoint at least one executor to carry out the instructions in your Will; it is usual to appoint two. Two executors should be appointed if the Will contains a gift to children who may be under 18 when you die. You should consider also appointing a substitutional executor in case one of the named executors is unable to act at the time of your death.

Appointing an executor does not make that person a beneficiary under your Will. You are only granting that person power to administer your estate. If you want to make the executor a beneficiary as well, you must do so in the part of your Will that deals with beneficiaries.

Since the primary duty of your executor is to carry out the terms of your Will, he or she must be responsible. You are trusting this person to act in the best interests of your estate. Your executors will usually be the trustees of any trust set up for your children. It is also desirable that at least one executor knows the beneficiaries personally. Often the person who stands to benefit most from your Will is appointed as one executor, with another relative or close friend as the second executor, who may assist or take over should the first be unable to act. A person cannot act as executor whilst under 18.

The duties of an executor need not be difficult, and your executor can use a solicitor to process the necessary probate forms. An executor is responsible for collecting in the deceased's assets, paying all debts and liabilities, including any Inheritance Tax due and distributing legacies to the correct beneficiaries. Examples of the sort of tasks which an executor may have to perform are:

1. Keeping assets in the estate.

2. Receiving assets from others.

3. Performing or refusing to perform the deceased's contracts.

4. Fulfilling charitable pledges made by the deceased.

5. Depositing or investing the estate's assets in appropriate investments.

6. Acquiring, abandoning or selling assets of the estate.

7. Subdividing, developing or improving land.

8. Leasing from or to others with an option to purchase.

9. Voting securities in person or by proxy.

10. Insuring assets against damage, loss and liability.

11. Insuring himself or herself against liability to others.

12. Borrowing money for the estate, with or without security, to be repaid from the estate's assets.

13. Paying taxes.

14. Selling share rights.

15. Employing people.

16. Consenting to the reorganisation, merger or winding up of a business.

17. Selling, mortgaging or leasing property in the estate.

18. Going to court to protect the estate from the claims of others.

19. Holding property in trust.

20. Paying funeral, administration and other costs.

21. Distributing the assets of the estate.

When all liabilities have been paid and all distributions have been made to the named beneficiaries the administration of the estate is complete. The executors' job is now finished. An executor must remain as a trustee if money is being held until a minor reaches the age of contingency, which may be 18 years or older.

It is not essential to check with your proposed executors in advance that they are willing to act. Unless contrary provisions are made in the Will, an executor may not charge any fees. However, lost work time and out-of-pocket expenses incurred in the administration of the estate may be reimbursed.

If you consider it appropriate, send a letter to your executors (see page 166) to notify them of their appointment. It contains the information they will normally need on their appointment concerning your Will. Do not attempt to include other instructions to your executors in this letter.

Naming a guardian for your children

If you have minor children, *England and Wales Will Forms 2* and *3* and *Scotland Will Forms 2* and *3* (see completed examples on pages 158-9 and 162-5) allow you to name a guardian to care for them in the event that they are left without a parent. Since a guardian takes the place of a parent, choose someone who can offer the best care for your children, such as a close relative who is willing to accept the responsibility. The guardian can also be one of your executors. Ideally, you should appoint two guardians, for example, a married couple or a guardian and a substitute guardian, to cover the possibility of one person being unable to serve upon your death.

There will be complications, and we advise you to consult a solicitor if any of the following occurred:

- You were not married to the other parent when the child was born.

- You and the other parent have already been or are (after the making of the Will) divorced from each other.

- There is or will be a court order stating where the child is to live or who has parental responsibility for the child.

A parent who does not have parental rights or has been deprived of such rights cannot appoint a guardian.

If in doubt, you are advised to see a solicitor.

Chapter 5:
Making your bequests

It is always best to draft your Will as simply as possible and in plain English. Avoid the use of legal words and phrases if you do not understand precisely what they mean. You must pay particular attention to the language of your bequests. A bequest is a gift in a Will of either money or property. For example, if you state 'I leave my watch to my daughter', you clearly know which watch and daughter you are referring to, but would this be clear to someone else? You may have the diamond-studded Rolex in mind and have forgotten about the broken Timex sitting in your desk drawer. You should describe the exact watch and the daughter who is to receive it.

How to say what you really mean

The language you use in your Will establishes your intentions. The more specific the language, the clearer your intentions will be to others. Do not use words such as *desire, hope, want, pray, would like, believe* or *request* when making your bequests. These are not words of intent; they simply reflect your wishes. Use as much detail when describing your property as is necessary to identify it. If you want to give a bequest unconditionally, state that you give the bequest 'absolutely'.

The following request may be too vague:

I give my collection of books to my sister Alice Smith.

Unless you want your sister to inherit every single book in your house, you have to be more specific. A clearer statement of your intentions might be:

I give my collection of 50 leatherbound first editions located in the oak bookcase under the window in my study to my sister Alice Smith.

In this case, your sister would only inherit 50 valuable volumes.

When describing buildings and land, give the name of the house (if any) and the address, or the property description, in as much detail as possible.

Be careful when using words that indicate quantity. Words such as *all*, *every* and *entire* mean there are no exceptions. Words such as *some, few* and *several* have no precise meaning other than to indicate that you mean more than one. Try to specify the number of items whenever possible.

If you mention your children consider whether you should name them (when any children born later may be excluded), or use some phrase as 'all my children living at my death' (which would include any children born after you make your Will and also any children who are conceived but not as yet born at the time of your death).

Since many charities and organisations have similar names, the beneficiary of a charitable bequest should be specifically identified.

'I give £2,000 to the Cancer Foundation' is an unclear bequest. You should identify this charity by its exact address. If you wish your bequest to go to a special fund within the charity, you must clearly identify that fund, such as library fund, research fund, building fund or educational fund.

Consider listing an alternative charity in the event of a specific charity no longer existing at the time of your death. Otherwise, you may indicate a general charitable purpose in your Will. This transfers your bequest to another charity with similar intentions and aims.

In the case of specific gifts, always indicate clearly who is to receive each item of property. Give names in full and identify each item of property clearly:

> *I give my stamp collection to my son Alexander Guy Ross*

or

> *I give my Rolex watch to my son James Ross.*

It is also possible to make a gift of money in a Will. This is usually called a 'legacy' or a 'pecuniary legacy'. Again, clearly indicate the amount and the person who is to receive it:

> *I give £1,000 to my son James Ross.*

In England and Wales, land bequeathed in a Will is divided into freehold and leasehold property. In Scotland, land ownership is usually akin to freehold.

Freehold property

This is land that you own absolutely. Absolute ownership means that, as sole owner of the land, you have the unconditional right to dispose of it in any manner, including leaving it in your Will. Any crops or grazing animals found on agricultural land pass with the land unless separate provisions are made in the Will.

Leasehold property

You may bequeath a lease of land in your Will. However, the executor may require permission from the freehold or absolute owner (or lessor) before he or she can assign the benefit of the lease to the beneficiary. There may be a clause in your lease prohibiting assignment of that lease without first obtaining permission from the freehold or absolute owner (or lessor) of the property.

Sometimes a particular item is charged with payment of a debt or other liability. In the case of land and buildings, such a charge is usually called a 'mortgage', but the widest term for such a charge is 'encumbrance'. If you are bequeathing property that has a debt against it, you should clearly indicate whether the person who receives the property takes it subject to the debt or encumbrance or free from the debt or encumbrance (in which case the debt or encumbrance will be paid out of the residue of the estate).

For example:

> I give to my daughter Mary Jane Ross my house at 5 Maple Terrace, London, SW10 2PZ, subject to the mortgage on it

or

> I give to my friend Diana Jenkins my shares in British Gas plc free from all encumbrances.

Specific gifts and legacies

You have the option of making specific gifts of individual items to named beneficiaries. These gifts of identifiable items owned by you, such as a particular gold ring, are called 'specific legacies' or 'specific bequests'. Gifts that do not necessarily form part of your estate, but which you would like someone to receive from the proceeds, are called 'general legacies'. Gifts of money are called 'pecuniary legacies'. In England and Wales, gifts of land are called 'devises'.

Specific legacies are distributed before pecuniary legacies. If there is not enough money in the estate to pay expenses and costs, general legacies and money bequeathed in the Will as pecuniary legacies must be used to satisfy those liabilities before specific legacies are used. As a result, there may be less money to distribute to your beneficiaries than originally planned.

Consider any specific gift carefully. Are there family heirlooms that would have a special meaning to someone? Do you want to leave a particular item to a nephew, for example? If you are a mother, would you not prefer to leave your jewellery to your daughter? A specific gift may not necessarily have monetary importance, but may have personal significance.

Forgiving debts

A Will may be used to cancel a debt owed to you by one of your beneficiaries. There are three ways to do this.

1. You may use your Will to release the person from his or her obligation to repay you, whether or not the person is left property. Simply state in the bequest section of your Will something that might read like this:

    I formally release John Smith from his obligation to repay any outstanding balance remaining on the £10,000 that I loaned him on 1ˢᵗ April, 1995.

2. Although John Smith owes you money, you may still want to leave him a bequest. If you want him to receive his full share of the bequest, insert a clause that might read like this:

    I bequeath £20,000 to John Smith and release him from his obligation to repay any money that he owes me. He is to receive the full amount of his bequest.

3. John Smith owes you money and you want your estate to be repaid. To accomplish this, make the bequest and deduct the outstanding debt from it. For example:

    I leave £10,000 to John Smith, less such balance on the £5,000 loan he owes me.

    If John Smith still owed you £3,000, he would receive only £7,000 from your £10,000 bequest. The remaining £3,000 in your estate would become part of the residuary gift and would be inherited by the beneficiary of that gift.

Your Will needs to be clear and precise on these matters. There are issues that may arise, for example, between parents and their children. If you give £5,000 to your son during your lifetime, is it a gift or a loan? This question needs to be resolved, since your son may be a beneficiary under your Will.

Gifts to minor children

A child under 18 cannot legally hold property that is left to him or her under a Will. The property will instead be held in trust for the child until the age of 18 (or a later age if specified). Moreover, you will not normally want your minor children to take outright immediately on your death. You are therefore asked in *England and Wales Will Forms 2* and *3* and *Scotland Will Forms 2* and *3* (see completed examples on pages 158-9 and 162-5) to state the age at which you want your children to inherit the capital, as opposed to the income, of your estate. Common ages to choose are 18, 21 or 25.

Before the child attains the age you specify, in England and Wales (but not in Scotland) your trustees have a statutory power to advance to the child up to half of the capital of the child's inheritance, or to use the capital for the child's benefit, but will do so only if they believe it is justified. A Will can enlarge this power. In Scotland, it would be normal to give your trustees power to pay income (and sometimes capital also) for the maintenance, education and benefit of the child prior to the child acquiring a right to the income or capital.

In England and Wales (but not in Scotland unless provided for in the Will) whilst the child is under 18, the trustees have discretion to use the income from the inheritance for the child's maintenance, education and benefit, or to accumulate the income by adding it to the capital. In this book's Will Form examples, any child has the right to all the income from the inheritance after reaching 18, whether or not you specify a greater age for inheriting the capital.

The residuary gift clause

'Residue' is the term used to describe what is left of your estate after the deduction of specific gifts, debts, legacies, taxes and administration expenses.

The residuary gift clause is often called a 'safety net' because it accounts for assets that might fall through the cracks in your Will. If you forgot to include a valuable piece of jewellery in your bequests, or you received a valuable painting after you prepared your Will, these overlooked assets would be distributed as though you had no Will if there was no residuary gift clause. But by using the residuary gift clause, you may designate exactly who is to receive any assets you may have overlooked.

If you do not use the residuary gift clause, assets not considered to be of a personal nature are sold and the proceeds are used to cover the cost of administering the estate and to pay monetary gifts. Anything left over is distributed according to the rules of intestacy outlined in Chapter 1. This could result in property distribution you may not want.

If you decide to make no specific gifts but instead give all your property as a single gift to one beneficiary, then this gift becomes the residuary gift, and the beneficiary receives whatever is left after the necessary deductions have been made.

Your residuary gift can be given to any number of beneficiaries. If it is given to more than one, you must state the share of the residue that each beneficiary is to receive. For example:

I give the residue of my estate to David Peter Ross, Susanna Hill and Nigel Jones in equal shares

or

I give the residue of my estate to my wife, Gillian Ross (two-thirds share), and to my brother Richard Ross (one-third share).

If you provide for a beneficiary to receive a particular proportion (for example, one third) you should ensure that it is clear what happens to that particular proportion if the beneficiary fails to survive.

Disposal of property during your lifetime

People often believe that once they leave property under their Will, they lose the right to sell or otherwise dispose of the property during their lifetime. This is not so. You retain the right to do whatever you choose with your property notwithstanding its mention in your Will.

For example:

I give my house, 5 Maple Terrace, London, SW10 2PZ, to my friend Peter Harrison

means that your friend Peter inherits 5 Maple Terrace only if you own it at the time of your death. If you sell it and buy another house, your friend would not receive the new house in its place.

Obviously, if your Will includes many bequests that are no longer possible to give because you no longer possess the items, it is time to prepare a new Will to dispose of the assets you do have.

What cannot be done in a Will?

The law governs a Will both during your lifetime and after your death.

- You cannot use your Will to libel or defame another person. If you write a false statement about another person and it becomes a matter of public record, as a Will does, your estate may be liable for damages. Do not try to damage another person's reputation through your Will.

- You cannot require someone to commit an act that is illegal in order to inherit under your Will. A Will cannot be used to violate public policy, such as requiring or forbidding a beneficiary to marry, work or have children. For example, if you leave money in your Will to establish a training school for pickpockets, or if in England and Wales (but probably not in Scotland) you leave money to your son on the condition that he divorce his wife, you have made illegal bequests.

- You cannot avoid a legal contract by a statement in a Will. If you had exchanged contracts to sell your home and you died before completion, the buyer could nevertheless enforce the contract.

- You cannot 'bequeath' one of your children, although you can express your wish as to whom you would want to be guardian of your child.

Special considerations

- **Insurance policies** – If your insurance policy does not have a specified beneficiary and there are no restrictions in your policy, you may, through your Will, leave the proceeds to anyone you choose.

- **Shares** – Shares may be disposed of in your Will subject to restrictions from the issuing company. Review your shareholdings regularly in case there are changes to the shares or capital of the companies in question.

- **Organs** – If you choose to be an organ donor, it is important that someone be appointed to authorise the organ removal shortly after death, as time is critical. By the time the Will is read it may be too late. Should you decide to leave your body to medical research, contact a local medical school or hospital to make the appropriate general arrangements.

Tax considerations

There may be income tax and capital gains tax liability arising prior to the date of death. All items of your estate are revalued at the date of death but there is no capital gains tax liability arising from such a revaluation. On large estates there may be an inheritance tax liability as well.

Generally, however, your estate will have no inheritance tax liability:

- on anything given to your spouse or to a charity.

- as long as the value of your estate is less than £255,000 (current figure), excluding anything given to your spouse or a charity and you have not made any gifts in the seven years before your death (and no other estate requires to be aggregated with your personal estate).

- on anything given more than seven years before your death.

- on gifts made before your death if they did not, in total, exceed £3,000 in any one tax year. Anything given to your spouse or a charity is not included in the calculation.

This book does not offer detailed tax advice; you should seek professional advice on tax matters. Moreover, because tax laws and rates do change, you are advised to review your Will at least once a year to take advantage of these changes.

Chapter 6:
Property that does not pass under your Will

Certain property does not pass under a Will and is not subject to probate (or Confirmation).

Is your house jointly owned with another person? If so, is the property held in England and Wales under a 'joint tenancy' or under a 'tenancy in common', or in Scotland under a 'survivorship destination' or 'jointly owned in shares'? If you are uncertain how your property is held, you should consult a solicitor.

If the property is held jointly under a joint tenancy (England & Wales) or with a survivorship destination (Scotland), you both own the whole property and upon your death your interest in the property automatically goes to your surviving co-owner, regardless of what the Will says. Such property owned jointly under a joint tenancy or with a survivorship destination does not pass under your Will.

However, if your property is owned jointly under a tenancy in common (England & Wales) or without a survivorship destination (Scotland), where you each own a specified share in the property, say half and half or one-third and two-thirds, you may give your share in the property to whomever you wish through your Will. Such property owned jointly under a tenancy in common or without a survivorship destination passes under your Will.

In England and Wales if you wish to do so, you can easily change a joint tenancy into a tenancy in common by presenting your co-owner with written notice of your intention. It is important, however, that this written notice be given before your death, not in your Will. In Scotland, you may not, without the consent of your co-owner, be able to defeat a survivorship destination.

In England & Wales, if you want to change a tenancy in common into a joint tenancy, you should see a solicitor.

Property owned jointly under a joint tenancy or under a survivorship destination is included as part of your estate for inheritance tax purposes. A surviving joint tenant (in England & Wales) or an individual holding property under a survivorship destination (in Scotland) is liable to pay any tax that may be due on inheriting your share of the jointly owned property, unless you specify otherwise. This does not apply to spouses. If you do not wish the other joint tenant or survivor to pay this tax personally, you must include the following statement in your Will:

> *I wish the burden of any tax due on my interest in property held under a* [*joint tenancy* (for England & Wales)][*survivorship destination* (for Scotland)] *to fall on my residuary estate.*

Generally, life insurance policies that are expressed to be for the benefit of your spouse, children or another named beneficiary do not pass under your Will. A life insurance policy is a good way to provide your family with the funds to meet any inheritance tax payable upon your death.

The premiums paid on such a life insurance policy may not be taxable if paid out of normal disposable income. The policy can be written in such a way that the proceeds are not taxable when you die. Consult your life insurance company for more details.

Your pension rights may pass outside your Will in the same way. Your employer should have more details. In many cases, you will be able to name the person who is to benefit from your pension rights, but only in a separate document, not in your Will.

Property which is situated abroad may not pass under your Will. You should consult a solicitor if you own or have an interest in property abroad.

Chapter 7: Frequently asked questions about bequests

Q. Suppose I accidentally bequeath more than I have?

A. Since it is impossible to give what you do not own, your beneficiaries will receive less than you had anticipated, or, depending upon the nature of the property and the costs and expenses associated with administering your estate, perhaps nothing at all.

Q. What happens if at the time of my death I no longer own property left in my Will?

A. If you have disposed of property and not updated your Will to reflect this change, the gift in your Will is 'adeemed', or cancelled. Such gifts can be adeemed in two ways:

1. You may have given the gift to the beneficiary during your lifetime. This is known as cancellation by satisfaction.

2. You may no longer own the property because you have sold it, given it away to someone other than the named beneficiary, or it has been destroyed. This is known as cancellation by extinction.

Q. What happens if my beneficiary dies before I do?

A. If a beneficiary predeceases you, your gift lapses, that is, the bequest has no effect and falls into the residue of your estate to be inherited by your residuary beneficiary. There are certain exceptions to this rule, the most important being that a gift to one of your children who dies before you may not lapse if that child leaves children of his or her own; the gift may instead go to those children. To prevent a possible lapse, you should name a substitutional beneficiary, or otherwise designate what should happen to the gift if the beneficiary predeceases you. However, if you predecease a beneficiary who then dies before the bequest is actually distributed, the beneficiary's estate inherits the property.

Q. What happens if my spouse and I die at the same time?

A. Usually, each spouse names the other as residuary beneficiary, thereby leaving the bulk of the estate to the other. However, situations such as car accidents sometimes claim both lives simultaneously.

In case it is impossible to determine who died first, the Will should contain a 'survivorship clause' specifying how the property is to be distributed. If the Will contains no such clause, it is assumed for the purposes of distribution that the elder spouse died first. If the elder spouse had no Will and dies intestate, the couple's estates will each be treated as if the other had died first.

If a husband survives his wife even by a few hours, he may die at least partially intestate, as he has lost his primary beneficiary. The distribution of property would follow the laws of intestacy. Since this may not coincide with your wishes, it would be better to include a survivorship clause in your Will specifically designating what is to happen to your property if your spouse does not survive you. Your spouse should likewise include a similar provision in his or her Will. Survivorship clauses are described in more detail in the next chapter.

Chapter 8:
Gifts and substitutional beneficiaries

If a beneficiary to whom you have given a specific gift or legacy dies before you, that gift will pass instead to your residuary beneficiary.

If your residuary beneficiary dies before you, the gift cannot pass to anyone else and there may be a partial intestacy. It is wise, therefore, to name an alternative or substitutional beneficiary who will take the residuary beneficiary's gift if he or she dies before you. Doing this avoids the possibility of partial intestacy, and gives you greater control over the destiny of your property.

Although it may be unlikely, it is also possible for a residuary beneficiary to die at the same time as you or very shortly after you, sometimes as a result of an accident affecting both of you. Your residue may pass to the residuary beneficiary and then almost immediately pass on, either under the beneficiary's Will or, if none, under the rules of intestacy, and again result in a distribution you may not have wanted. The inclusion of a survivorship clause prevents this process and allows you to decide who will inherit your property. The survivorship period can be any length of time, but it is common to choose 28 days; a period of longer than six months can have tax consequences and also hold up the distribution of the estate.

Example:

> I give the residue of my estate to my wife, Gillian Ross, but if she fails to survive me by 28 days or if this gift fails for any reason, I give the residue to my brother Richard Ross.

The survivorship clause by its nature also covers the event of the residuary beneficiary predeceasing you. The book's completed examples of *England and Wales Will Forms 1 and 2* and *Scotland Will Forms 1 and 2* contain survivorship clauses.

If you give your residue initially to more than one person in shares, you need to make clear whether, if one of them dies:

- that person's share goes to another person as substitutional beneficiary, or

- the share goes to the survivors of the people you named initially.

In sample *England and Wales Will Form 1* and *Scotland Will Form 1*, the residuary gift clause reads:

> *I GIVE the residue of my estate to*_____
> _____ *but if*
> *he/she or (if I have indicated more than one person) any of them fails to*
> *survive me by 28 days or if this gift or any part of it fails for any other*
> *reason, then I GIVE the residue of my estate or the part of it affected to*
> _____.

So if you name another person as substitutional beneficiary and any of the persons named initially dies, his or her share will pass to the substitutional beneficiary. However, if you have initially named more than one person, it may be unlikely that all of them will fail to survive you. If you want the share of any who dies to go to the others, you should write at the end of the Residuary Gift 'the other residuary beneficiary' if you initially named only two or 'the other residuary beneficiaries in proportion to their shares' if you initially named more than two.

Example:

> *I GIVE the residue of my estate to David Peter Ross, Susanna Hill and*
> *Nigel Jones in equal shares but if he/she or (if I have indicated more than one*
> *person) any of them fails to survive me by 28 days or if this gift or any part*
> *of it fails for any other reason, then I GIVE the residue of my estate or the*
> *part of it affected to the other residuary beneficiaries in proportion to their*
> *shares.*

In *England and Wales Will Form 2* and *Scotland Will Form 2*, if you name two or more adults to take initially and one dies, his or her share will go to their children.

If this is not what you want, or if any of the above is not clear, you should see a solicitor.

Substitutional gifts after gifts to children

In the case of gifts to children, the position is different. In *England and Wales Will Forms 2 and 3* and *Scotland Will Forms 2 and 3* of this book you are asked to state the age at which you want the children to inherit the capital of your estate. A child who is living at your death and has attained the stated age will inherit immediately. If living at your death but not yet of the stated age, the child will inherit on reaching that age. In England and Wales a child can never hold property in his or her own name before the age of 18. In Scotland, if property is held in the name of a child under the age of 18 a problem may arise if and when the child wants to dispose of the property before the age of 18.

If a child dies without leaving children, whether before or after your death but under the stated age, *England and Wales Will Forms 2 and 3* and *Scotland Will Forms 2 and 3* ensure that the share the child would have taken goes to increase the shares of your other children.

If, on the other hand, a child dies under the stated age leaving his or her own children (your grandchildren), different rules apply. *England and Wales Will Forms 2 and 3* and *Scotland Will Forms 2 and 3* make clear what is to happen with the following words:

> *... if any of my children dies before me or after me but under that age, I GIVE the share that child would have taken to his or her own children who attain 18 equally.*

Taking the completed examples of *England and Wales Will Form 2* and *Scotland Will Form 2*, the residue will go:

1. to Gillian's husband, David, if he survives her by 28 days, but if he dies before that,

then

2. equally among such of Gillian's children, Mary, James and Alexander, who outlive Gillian and reach the age of 21, jointly with the issue who survive and attain the age of 21 of any of Gillian's children who may have predeceased or failed to attain 21.

If, for example, Mary dies under that age, James and Alexander will take Mary's share (in other words they each will get half) unless Mary has children who survive her and Gillian and attain 18; in that case, Mary's children will get their mother's share and James and Alexander will still get one-third each,

but

3. to Theresa Mundy if none of the beneficiaries under number 2 (above) lives to the necessary age. In other words, Theresa acts as a long-stop beneficiary if none of Gillian's children or grandchildren inherits under these provisions.

It is wise to see a solicitor if one of your children is already dead when you make your Will but grandchildren survive.

Chapter 9:
Safe-keeping of your Will

After completion, your Will should be kept in a safe place: either at home with your other important legal documents or lodged with a bank or solicitor. Your Will must be immediately available upon your death. If it cannot be found, the court may determine it to have been intentionally destroyed by you and your property will be distributed according to the laws of intestacy.

It is important in England and Wales that you do not staple, clip or attach any other documents to your Will. Make sure your executors and a member of your family know of its whereabouts. It is sensible to keep a letter or note with your private papers as to where your Will is held. It may be appropriate to keep a photocopy of your Will in case the original is accidentally lost or destroyed, but it should be clear that it is only a copy.

Should you decide to deposit your Will with your bank, it may be wise to introduce your executor to the bank officer responsible for providing access to the Will. By doing this, you can avoid delays when it is time to retrieve the Will.

Alternatively, your original Will in England and Wales may be deposited at the Probate Registry. This has several advantages, the most important being that your Will is guaranteed to be held securely. Since your Will is recorded, no attempt can be made to administer your estate by bypassing your Will. (There is no official depository in Scotland.)

The filing fee is currently £15, and the Probate Registry personnel will give you a special envelope for your Will. Place your Will inside, seal it and write your name and the names, addresses and other information about the executors on the outside. Sign the envelope in front of a witness or an officer of the Probate Registry. You may either hand-deliver this envelope with your Will to the Probate Registry or sub-office or send it by registered post with a covering letter.

In return, you will receive a registration certificate. This is your proof that your Will has been deposited with the Probate Registry. Notify your executors immediately.

A Citizens Advice Bureau can direct you to the nearest Probate Registry. You may also be able to find the address in the telephone directory or Yellow Pages.

Part 2

Power of Attorney & Living Will

Chapter 10: What is a Power of Attorney?

A Power of Attorney is the formal, written authority granted by one person (the 'Donor' in England and Wales or the 'Granter' in Scotland) to another person (the 'Attorney') enabling the Attorney to act on the Donor's/Granter's behalf and manage his or her financial interests.

This book deals with two kinds of Powers of Attorney: (i) General (GPA) and (ii) Enduring (EPA) which is applicable in England and Wales, otherwise called Continuing (CPA) in Scotland. To prevent confusion, we will refer to both EPAs and CPAs as 'EPAs' in the following chapters. Should a CPA be referred to specifically, then the Scots law applies.

A General Power of Attorney is a relatively straightforward authorisation for wide-ranging use for specific periods or events. The need to create a General Power might arise, for example, if you go abroad and need to entrust the management of business interests to your spouse.

Enduring Powers of Attorney are rather more complicated to create and administer than General Powers for the simple reason that they remain valid in the event of the Donor becoming mentally incapable of handling his or her own affairs, and so require particular procedures and formalities to be followed. A General Power on the other hand is automatically revoked if the Donor becomes mentally incapable.

The actual scope and nature of an Attorney's power under an EPA and a General Power are broadly the same. The General Power or EPA can define and restrict the authority given. An EPA provides a way of allowing there to be long-term control of a Donor's interests, albeit in the hands of others, particularly if he or she is elderly or in poor health.

This book contains completed examples of one *General Power of Attorney Form* for use in England and Wales and one for Scotland. Instructions for their completion can be found in chapter 15. Chapters 11-14 deal solely with aspects of creating and administering an EPA or CPA.

How EPAs are different

Unlike a General Power, an EPA remains effective *after* the Donor has become mentally incapable of managing his or her own affairs.

To be valid an EPA must have been granted by the Donor whilst he or she was still mentally capable. In England and Wales, when the Attorney believes the Donor is or may soon become incapable, he or she must:

1.   Give notice to the Donor of his or her intention to apply to register the EPA with an office of the Supreme Court called the Court of Protection (the role of the Court of Protection, as defined by the Mental Health Act 1983, is to safeguard the property and affairs of people with mental disability).

2.   Give notice of his or her intention to certain of the Donor's nearest relatives.

3.   Apply to the Court of Protection to register the EPA.

Until the EPA is registered and full power is restored, the Attorney will have limited authority. Please refer to chapter 14 for a detailed discussion on the registration procedure.

In Scotland, a CPA must be registered with the Office of the Public Guardian (OPG). Registration is discussed in chapter 14.

The benefits of an EPA

If you were to become ill or disabled without an EPA and were unable to manage your financial affairs yourself, no one could act on your behalf unless he or she first went to court for either (a) the appointment of your Receiver by the Court of Protection in England and Wales, or (b) authority to deal with your affairs in Scotland.

Even your spouse and children may be powerless to act on your behalf. Although courts will appoint someone to act for you and to protect your interests, this is not always a desirable alternative for three reasons:

1.   **The delay.** It can take several weeks or even months to have someone appointed who will have the authority to make legal, financial and business decisions for the Donor. With an EPA the Attorney can act for the Donor immediately. The continued control of your interests is thus maintained by someone you have chosen.

2. **Selection of Attorney.** When someone is ill or disabled they lose the ability to select their Attorney. The court may or may not appoint as Receiver (in England and Wales) or grant authority to (in Scotland) the person the Donor would have preferred.

3. **Advantages of immediate and lasting delegation.** In England and Wales, from the date on which the EPA is signed by the Attorney (see chapter 13) or in Scotland from the date on which the CPA is signed by the Donor and registered, the Attorney has authority to act on behalf of the Donor unless this power has been specifically restricted by the Donor. This means that the Donor can take advantage of being able to delegate responsibilities if, for example, he or she goes on holiday.

Must the EPA be in a particular form?

Yes. In England and Wales, the form of an EPA differs significantly from the relatively simple wording of a General Power. The Enduring Powers of Attorney (Prescribed Form) Regulations 1990 require that all EPAs follow a specific form, as contained in this book (see pages 167-70 for a completed example). The form must include explanatory information which you will see in Part A and in all the relevant marginal notes to parts B and C. You should read this information carefully.

In Scotland, the Adults with Incapacity (Scotland) Act 2000 and The Adults with Incapacity (Certificates in relation to Powers of Attorney) (Scotland) Regulations 2001 require certain provisions to be included in the CPA and each CPA requires a Certificate in stated form to be used.

The notes included in the EPA form are designed to make clear to both the Donor and the Attorney the extent and nature of the Attorney's powers and duties. This is particularly important in England and Wales because the Attorney has a duty to register the EPA as soon as it becomes clear that the Donor is, or will soon be, incapable of acting on his or her own behalf.

An EPA must include statements:

(i) by the Donor, to show that he or she intends the power to continue in spite of any subsequent mental incapacity of his or hers;

(ii) by the Donor to show that he or she has read or has had read to him or her the information explaining the effect of creating the power; and

(iii) in England and Wales by the Attorney to show that he or she understands the duty of registration imposed by the Enduring Powers of Attorney Act 1985 and in Scotland in the CPA registration application form by the Attorney to show that he or she is willing to act as Attorney.

When does the EPA become effective?

The Donor needs to establish when he can rely on the Attorney to handle his or her affairs. The Attorney must be aware of when the power begins and ends so that he or she will meet his or her responsibilities and not exceed the authority. Third parties need to know when they can and should reasonably rely upon and deal with the Attorney.

In England and Wales, if there is no indication to the contrary, the EPA will begin immediately after it has been signed by the Donor and the Attorney. However, the Donor may wish to restrict the power by stating that it should not begin until the Donor is incapable of acting on his or her own behalf. The easiest way to establish that condition is by stating in the power that it is not to be used by the Attorney until the need arises to apply for registration.

In Scotland, in order to be effective the CPA needs to be registered with the Office of the Public Guardian (OPG). The CPA can be used immediately after it has been signed by the Granter and registered with the OPG.

In England and Wales, the Donor can revoke the EPA at any time before it has been registered, as long as he or she is still mentally capable. After the EPA has been registered, it is up to the Court of Protection to cancel registration and revoke the EPA (see page 63).

In Scotland, the Donor can revoke the CPA at any time after it has been registered, as long as he or she is still mentally capable. If you wish to do so, you should consult a solicitor to draft a Deed of Revocation. Furthermore, in Scotland a CPA will be terminated (a) where the Donor and the Attorney are married to each other, upon the granting of a Decree of Separation or divorce to either party or a declarator of nullity of marriage, unless the CPA states otherwise, or (b) on the appointment of a guardian with powers related to those conferred in the CPA.

Chapter 11:
EPA: the Donor

Granting an EPA allows the Donor to select the person most suitable to protect his or her interests, so a Donor should consider the implications and practicalities of granting such a power. A Donor should be open and communicative with his or her Attorney.

Who may be a Donor and make an EPA?

Any individual who is aged 18 or over, has sufficient mental capacity and is not an undischarged bankrupt can make an EPA. A company or a partnership cannot make an EPA.

Two or more Donors cannot make a joint EPA appointing the same Attorney. Donors must make individual powers and the EPA will not be accepted for registration unless this is complied with.

What does 'sufficient mental capacity' mean?

In England and Wales, for the purpose of the Attorney registering an EPA, a Donor's 'mental incapacity' is clearly defined in the Enduring Power of Attorney Act 1985 as being 'incapable by reason of mental disorder of managing and administering [one's own] property and affairs'.

There is, however, no express definition of mental capacity to grant an EPA or CPA. To have the mental capacity to be the Donor of an EPA, you must be capable of understanding the nature and effect of the powers granted at the time you make the EPA.

It is not necessary that the Donor be capable of performing all the acts which the EPA authorises, but the Donor cannot authorise the Attorney to do something which he himself is not legally entitled to do. For example, it is possible that someone suffering from mental illness might be incapable of handling transactions, but capable of understanding the process and consequences of granting an EPA. Similarly, an EPA is valid if a mentally ill person executed it during a period of lucidity. However, if the EPA is made under such circumstances, it would be advisable to obtain medical evidence of the Donor's mental capacity at the time of making the EPA. This could later be needed as evidence of the EPA's validity if there is an objection raised by, for example, one of the Donor's relatives.

What kind of authority can a Donor give in an EPA?

When a Donor makes an EPA, he or she can state what kind of authority the Attorney may have. This can be:

1. A general authority; this means that the Attorney will be able to do anything which the Donor is or was legally able to do.

2. A specific authority; this means that the Donor states the specific acts which he or she has delegated to the Attorney. The Attorney will only have authority for that specific matter.

3. A general or specific authority which has been restricted in some way by the Donor. For example, the Donor does not want the EPA to have immediate effect but wants it to become effective only when he or she has actually become mentally incapable.

Choosing your Attorney or Attorneys

A Donor may appoint one Attorney or more than one. Careful thought should be given when choosing your Attorney, since this person will be dealing closely with your personal affairs. In England and Wales, when the Attorney applies to register the EPA (see chapter 14), the Court has the right to refuse to register the power if it considers the Attorney(s) to be unsuitable. Also consider who would be a practical choice of Attorney. Someone living abroad, for example, would not be able to deal with your affairs easily.

If you appoint more than one Attorney, you must decide how they are to act. They may act either:

1. 'jointly', which means they must all act together and cannot act separately. If one of the joint Attorneys disclaims, dies, becomes bankrupt or mentally incapable, the joint appointment will terminate but in Scotland you can provide that the survivor in a joint appointment may act; or

2. 'jointly and severally', which means they may act together, but also separately if they want to. If one of the Attorneys who has been appointed on a joint and several basis disclaims, dies, becomes bankrupt or mentally incapable, the power will not automatically be terminated as the other(s) can continue to act.

Many Donors appoint family members to be their Attorney(s). For example, they may appoint their spouse as Attorney together with their children, with an informal understanding that the children will not act while the spouse is able to do so.

Restrictions

When a Donor fills in the form to create an EPA, he or she has the opportunity to restrict the extent of the authority which the Attorney has, or to place limitations on dealing with certain parts of the Donor's property. He or she may also choose to appoint different Attorneys to deal with different parts of his or her property. Examples of common restrictions or limitations made by Donors are described below.

A Donor may grant more than one EPA to act concurrently with each other.

Postponing the 'start date' of the EPA

Some Donors may not want the EPA to be effective immediately, but would rather state that it should not come into effect until a time when the Donor has become mentally incapable. It may nevertheless be preferable to allow the EPA to be registered immediately albeit that the EPA would not be able to be used until the Donor had mental incapacity. This will mean that the Attorney would have powers whenever the Donor has become mentally incapable.

Restricting the scope of the Attorney's authority

The Donor may want to prevent the Attorney from dealing with a particular part of his or her property or affairs. If you wish to do something similar, you should take care to ensure that you have made other arrangements for the excluded property and that you have not left anything overlooked. Consult a solicitor if you have any doubts.

If the Donor is also a trustee

In England and Wales, if as a Donor you are a trustee and your Attorney is a beneficiary of the trust, but you do not want your Attorney to have the power to do anything you can do as a trustee, you should ask a solicitor to help you with your EPA. Bear in mind that co-ownership of a home involves trusteeship; if you do not restrict the EPA, you will delegate power to act in the trust of the jointly owned property to the Attorney if the Attorney is the co-owner. Even though an Attorney can do anything the Donor could do, in land law, if a sale is effected, the monies must be paid to two or more trustees; therefore an Attorney cannot act for himself and the Donor if he is the sole Attorney. So he would have to exercise his powers of appointment (as a trustee) to appoint another trustee to act jointly so that the monies can be correctly paid to two or more trustees. Power to exercise the Donor's trust functions in other circumstances can often be granted for no more than 12 months, but the rules are complicated and if it is important that the Attorney should have this power, legal advice should be taken.

In Scotland, a trustee is not permitted to pass his or her authority to act as trustee to another. Therefore the CPA will not authorise your Attorney to carry out any act for you in your capacity as trustee.

Making gifts

In England and Wales, Attorneys are permitted to make some gifts to certain people, including themselves (see pages 51 and 167). Some Donors choose to restrict this power, for example, stating that Attorneys should not be able to make gifts to themselves. More radical gifts would in any event require the consent of the Court of Protection if a good case could be made out.

In Scotland, only if specifically authorised to do so would Attorneys be permitted to make gifts whether to themselves or to others.

Duties of the Donor

If there are any restrictions on the Donor's power to grant an EPA he or she must specify these to the Attorney, or the Donor will be liable for any damages that result from his or her failure to do so. If, for example, the Attorney breaches a contract with a third party because the Donor did not inform him or her of the existence of that contract, the Donor, not the Attorney, will be liable for any damages sought by the third party.

If any Attorney's actions exceed the limits prescribed in the EPA, the Donor is not obliged to validate the Attorney's actions after those actions have taken place — the Attorney acted on his or her own accord. The Donor should, as mentioned above, make certain that the scope of the Attorney's power as indicated in the EPA is made sufficiently clear to prevent such an occasion from arising.

Revoking the EPA

In England and Wales, if a Donor changes his or her mind after the EPA has been signed, he or she can revoke the EPA at any time provided he or she is still mentally capable and the EPA has not yet been registered with the Court of Protection. If you want to do so, consult a solicitor who will draft a Deed of Revocation for you.

An EPA cannot be revoked once it has been registered unless and until the Court of Protection confirms the revocation. The Court will require medical evidence that the Donor is mentally capable, or was mentally capable at the time, when he or she revoked the EPA.

In Scotland, the Donor can revoke the CPA at any time after it has been registered as long as he or she is still mentally capable. If you want to do that you should consult a solicitor to draft a Deed of Revocation. Furthermore, a CPA will be terminated (a) where the Donor and the Attorney are married to each other, upon the granting of a Decree of Separation or divorce to either party or a declarator of nullity of marriage, unless the CPA states otherwise or (b) on the appointment of a guardian with powers related to those conferred in the CPA.

Chapter 12:
EPA: the Attorney

An Attorney is someone who has been chosen by the Donor to act on his or her behalf in financial matters. The Attorney will be able to do anything which the Donor could legally do, such as signing cheques or selling shares.

Who may be an Attorney?

Anyone who is willing, who is over 18 and who is not bankrupt when he or she signs the EPA can be an Attorney. A trust corporation, for example, a bank, can also be an Attorney.

Attorneys do not have to live in England, Wales or Scotland, but if resident abroad they may have difficulty in executing some of the transactions on the Donor's behalf.

Powers and duties of the Attorney

It is important that both the Donor and the Attorney clearly understand the powers and duties of the Attorney. It should be understood that, subject to the exceptions below and any restrictions placed on the power by the Donor, the Attorney can do anything the Donor can legally do. This might include, for example, preparing tax returns, making investment decisions, arranging insurance, employing staff or selling property. In England and Wales (but not in Scotland unless specifically authorised to do so), the Attorney also has the power to make gifts, although the law does limit the scope of this power.

In England and Wales (but not in Scotland unless specifically authorised to do so), an Attorney may make reasonable gifts (bearing in mind how much money the Donor has) to a charity or to an individual who is related to or connected to the Donor and to himself or herself as Attorney. However, the gifts must be of a seasonal nature, i.e. they must be at Christmas, for birthdays or wedding anniversaries.

What an Attorney cannot do under an EPA

The Attorney cannot:

(i) execute a Last Will & Testament on behalf of the Donor (however, in England or Wales, but not in Scotland, the Court may grant authority for doing so). In England and Wales, the Will-making procedure can take many months and can only be done after registration;

(ii) take any action concerning the Donor's marriage or divorce;

(iii) appoint a substitute or successor for himself or herself as an Attorney for the Donor;

(iv) decide questions of health care or welfare on behalf of the Donor.

Whether the EPA is general or specific and whether or not it is limited or restricted in any way, its wording must be strictly observed by the Attorney who must not act beyond the authority given by the Donor.

Registration

It is the Attorney's duty in England and Wales (but not in Scotland) to (i) notify the Donor and certain of the Donor's close relatives of his or her intention to register the EPA and to (ii) apply to register the EPA at the Court of Protection when he or she becomes aware that the Donor is, or may soon be, mentally incapable.

Please refer to chapter 14 for detailed instructions concerning the registration procedure.

The Attorney(s) should understand that, after they have notified the Donor and the relatives and applied for registration, they have only limited powers until the EPA is registered. The authority of the Attorney(s) to deal with the Donor's affairs during this time is limited to the maintenance of the Donor and preventing loss to his or her estate.

In Scotland, the CPA requires registration with the Office of the Public Guardian before it can be used but it is not necessary and it may indeed be inappropriate to notify relatives.

Standard of care

An Attorney must apply the same standard of care to duties as an Attorney as he or she would apply to addressing his or her own personal concerns. A professional Attorney (for example, a solicitor or a bank manager) must carry out the duties as a prudent businessperson acting as a trustee would do.

Example: When Margaret gave Joe the power to authorise repairs on her car she did not specify how this was to be done. It was Joe's duty to proceed in the most reasonable manner possible, i.e. by using a professional mechanic. When instead Joe sent the car to his 17-year-old neighbour who worked on cars as a weekend hobby, he was not proceeding reasonably or according to convention, and thus could have been liable for damages resulting from poor work on Margaret's car.

Disclosure of conflict

The Attorney must not undertake acts which conflict with his duties to another person and must disclose any such conflict of interest to the Donor. If he or she is aware that conflicts may arise, it would be better to refuse to act as Attorney in the first place.

Confidentiality

Unless the Donor authorises disclosure, the Attorney must keep the Donor's concerns confidential. He or she may not use his knowledge of the Donor's affairs to his or her own benefit or to the benefit of anyone else.

Accounts

It is advisable for the Attorney to keep complete, up-to-date records of transactions involving the Donor's money, and keep this money apart from his or her own.

Compensation for work done as an Attorney

Unless it is expressly specified in the EPA, the Attorney is generally not entitled to compensation, although he or she would be entitled to reimbursement for out-of-pocket expenses. If the Attorney is a professional, he or she may expect compensation and this should be agreed in advance of the appointment.

If your Attorney is also a trustee for you, the Attorney may not be allowed compensation as trustees are not allowed to profit from trusts unless it is expressly authorised by the trust.

Court of Protection

In England and Wales, the Court of Protection can impose additional duties on the Attorney, before registration of an EPA, as well as after, if it sees indications that the Donor is, or is about to be, mentally incapable. According to the Enduring Power of Attorney Act 1985, the Court has the authority to exercise the following prerogatives:

(i) to give directions as to the management or disposal by the Attorney of the Donor's property and affairs;

(ii) to direct the rendering of accounts by the Attorney, and the production of the records he or she keeps for that purpose;

(iii) to give directions regarding the Attorney's remuneration or expenses, whether or not they are mentioned in the EPA, including the power to make orders to repay excessive remuneration, or to pay additional sums;

(iv) to require that the Attorney furnish information or produce documents or things which he or she has in his or her possession in his or her capacity as Attorney;

(v) to give any consent or authority which the Attorney would have had to obtain from a mentally capable Donor;

(vi) to authorise the Attorney to benefit himself or herself, or persons other than the Donor, in some way beyond the general statutory authority.

Disclaiming the role of Attorney

An Attorney may decide that he or she no longer wishes to act as an Attorney. If the Attorney decides to disclaim the power whilst the Donor is still mentally capable (and in England and Wales the EPA has therefore not been registered), then the Attorney should give notice of his or her disclaimer to the Donor in writing. If the EPA has been registered, the Attorney should give notice in writing to the Court of Protection.

In Scotland, if and when an Attorney decides to disclaim the power under a CPA then the Attorney should give notice to the Office of the Public Guardian (as well as to the Donor if mentally capable).

Chapter 13:
How to prepare an EPA

For England and Wales

Preparing an EPA

An Enduring Power of Attorney form comprises Parts A, B and C. A completed example of this form has been included in this book for guidance, beginning on page 167.

Part A

This gives explanatory notes about filling in the form. Both the Donor and the Attorney(s) should read the notes carefully before signing the document.

Part B

This is the section of the form which must be completed by the Donor and it is here that any restrictions on the Power to be granted must be noted. Remember that there can only be one Donor per form.

Part C

This section of the form must be completed by the Attorney(s).

Completing the EPA

You should take care to express clearly in the EPA exactly what you want to authorise. Ambiguous wording can undermine an EPA, either by leading the Court to interpret limitations more narrowly than intended, or by allowing an Attorney to exceed the intended limits of the Power.

Example: When Priscilla gave Arthur 'the authority to make an annual gift to an organisation that works with wildlife', she intended that he make such gifts to an organisation that worked to preserve wildlife in its natural habitat. The last thing she wanted was what happened. Arthur misinterpreted her ambiguous wording and made a large contribution to the local zoo. The Court, however, found Arthur's interpretation to be a reasonable one, and the gift was made for each of the following five years.

The Court of Protection has the authority to resolve any question on the intent of a limited power. The Courts interpret limited Powers very strictly, so it is important that all wording in the EPA reflects the full intended scope of the Power. After the EPA is registered, the Donor can no longer extend the scope of the Power and can no longer validate acts that the Attorney has taken.

Filling in Part B of the form as a Donor

The Attorneys

You must name your Attorney(s) and decide whether you want them to act jointly or jointly and severally (see page 46). Remember to delete the statements which do not comply with your wishes.

The Nature of the Authority

You can give your Attorney(s) a general power or a specific power (see page 46 for details). If you want to give a specific power, you need to state what that is in the space provided. Similarly, you will have to decide whether the general or specific Power is in relation to all of your property and affairs or only part of them.

In both cases, remember to cross out all the alternatives which do not apply to you.

Restrictions

You may stipulate restrictions on the second page of Part B if you wish. For example, you may want to say that the EPA should not be effective until the need arises to apply for registration.

Registration

You will see that the second page of Part B includes a statement that you (the Donor) intend that the power will continue even if you become mentally incapable. You should understand that this means that your Attorney(s) is under an obligation to apply to register the EPA if he or she believes that you are or are becoming mentally incapable.

Filling in Part C of the form as an Attorney

If there is more than one Attorney, each of you should fill in a separate Part C.

You will see that the written instructions on the form state your obligation to apply for registration once the Donor is, or is becoming, mentally incapable. Please see chapter 14 for details on how to do this.

Signing the EPA

If the Donor is mentally capable and understands what the EPA is, he or she should sign the EPA in the presence of a witness, who should then sign his or her name and add his or her details in the space provided. The witness should not be one of the Attorneys or the Donor's spouse.

If the Donor is physically unable to sign or is illiterate, then he or she should make a mark and someone, who is not an Attorney or a witness, should sign on the Donor's behalf. A statement should then be put on the form to state that the EPA and explanatory information were read out to the Donor, who appeared to understand it fully. If someone signs on behalf of the Donor, then it should be done in the presence of two witnesses, who should then sign their names and add their details. If you have any doubts, consult a solicitor.

The Attorney(s) must sign the EPA after the Donor and should only sign if he or she believes the Donor has not already become mentally incapable. If there is more than one Attorney, they can sign on different days and with different witnesses at anytime after the Donor has signed the form. Remember that Attorneys must not witness each others' signature and a Donor must not witness an Attorney's signature. Please note that a blind person cannot act as a witness.

For Scotland

Preparing a CPA

A Continuing Power of Attorney gives wide authority without restriction or limitation. If restriction or limitation were required then it should be clearly stated at the end where provided.

You should take care to express clearly in the CPA exactly what you want to authorise; ambiguous wording can undermine a CPA.

The Attorneys

You must insert the full name and address of the Attorney (or Attorneys) and decide whether you want them to act jointly or jointly and severally (see page 46). Remember to delete the statements which do not comply with your wishes.

Signing the CPA

If the Donor is mentally capable and understands what the CPA is, he or she should sign the CPA in the presence of a witness, who should then sign his or her name and add his or her full name and address and occupation in the space provided. The witness should not be one of the Attorneys or the Donor's spouse.

The Certificate

A CPA requires an accompanying Certificate that must be in the prescribed form (see completed example on page 185). The appropriate Certificate for a CPA must be signed by a 'Prescribed Person' who can be either a solicitor, a practising member of the Faculty of Advocates or a registered medical practitioner. The Certificate states that the Prescribed Person has interviewed the Donor immediately before the Donor subscribed the CPA and has satisfied himself or herself that at the time the CPA is granted the Donor understands its nature and extent and that he or she has no reason to believe that the Donor is acting under undue influence, or that any other factor prevents the granting of the CPA.

The person who signs the required Certificate to accompany the CPA cannot be the Attorney.

Chapter 14: Registering the EPA

For England and Wales

Registering an EPA

It is the Attorney's duty to apply to the Court of Protection to register the EPA when he or she sees evidence that the Donor has become, or is becoming, mentally incapable. It is down to the Attorney's judgment as to when this happens. The Attorney may need to take medical advice about whether the Donor is or is not mentally incapable; but no proof is needed of the Donor's mental incapacity to register the power. However, if there is an objection raised to the proposed registration, the Court of Protection will require some medical evidence that the Donor is not mentally capable.

It is in everyone's interests to proceed with the registration as quickly as possible after the Donor has become mentally incapable.

Notification

Before making the application to the Court for the registration of the EPA, the Attorney(s) must give notice of the proposed registration to the Donor and certain close relatives of the Donor. All notices of intention to register the EPA must be made on the prescribed *Form EP1 Notice of intention to apply for registration*. Please see page 171 for completed example.

Notifying the relatives

Notice must be given by the Attorney(s) to at least three relatives of the Donor. Relatives are placed in classes and put in order of priority. If the requirement to give notice to three relatives means that one of a class is notified, then all people in that class must be notified.

For example:

1. The Donor has a wife, four sons and both parents still alive. The wife and sons would have to be notified.

2. The Donor is a widower with three daughters and two brothers. Only the three daughters would need to receive notification.

If the Donor does not have three living relatives who fall within the prescribed classes, the Attorney(s) should state that on the Application to Register.

Below are the relatives entitled to notice in the order in which they must be notified:

1. The Donor's husband or wife.

2. The Donor's children.

3. The Donor's parents.

4. The Donor's brothers and sisters, whether of the whole or half blood. A person is a relative of the whole blood to another if they share two common parents. A relative who shares only one common parent is a relative of the half blood.

5. The widow or widower of a child of the Donor.

6. The Donor's grandchildren.

7. The children of the Donor's brothers and sisters of the whole blood.

8. The children of the Donor's brothers and sisters of the half blood.

9. The Donor's uncles and aunts of the whole blood.

10. The children of the Donor's uncles and aunts of the whole blood.

A person is not entitled to notice if:

- his or her name or address is unknown to the Attorney

- he or she is less than 18 years of age

- he or she is mentally incapable

Notification of the relatives may be done by first-class post. It does not need to be done in person.

What if one or more of the Attorneys are also notifiable relatives?

This will often be the case, as many Donors choose to have their spouse or children as their Attorney(s). If any Attorneys are also notifiable relatives, then they can count themselves as having been notified and there is no need to fill in Form EP1. For example, if an Attorney is one of the Donor's three children and the Donor has no spouse, then only the two children who are not Attorneys need to be notified.

Notifying the Donor

The Attorney must give notice to the Donor in person by actually handing it to the Donor, even if the Donor appears not to realise what is happening. Notification to the Donor cannot be done by post.

Is it always necessary to give notice to the Donor and/to the relatives?

The law does allow exemptions from the requirement to give notice in exceptional circumstances, as many Attorneys find it distressing to have to inform Donors of their failing mental capacity. Application for dispensation from the requirement to serve notice on anyone entitled to receive it, including the Donor, can be made to the Public Trustee on *Form EP3 General form of application* (see completed example on page 179) and the original EPA should also be sent.

However, the Public Trustee is unlikely to give a dispensation unless the circumstances are truly exceptional as it is the Donor's right to be informed and to be able to object to the proposed registration. Dispensation will normally only be given where it can be shown that the Donor would be unduly harmed or distressed by the news.

Who should give the notices if there is more than one Attorney?

Attorneys appointed jointly must give notices jointly or they will not be deemed to be valid. If there is more than one Attorney appointed to act jointly and severally, then they should give the notices jointly if they both want to act following the registration of the power. If only one of them gives the notices, then the other(s) must also be sent *Form EP1*. If the notices of intention to register do not name all of the Attorneys, then registration will take place but will be limited to only those Attorneys whose names were on the *Form EP1*.

Application for registration

Who must apply?

If Attorneys have been appointed to act jointly, they must all apply for registration in order for the power to be valid. This is necessary because under a joint power the Attorneys cannot act without each other. If

Attorneys have been appointed to act jointly and severally, they do not all have to apply but only those who do will continue to have power.

In some cases more than one EPA or CPA may have been granted by one donor. In these cases each EPA or CPA must be registered separately.

The application form

The application to register the EPA must be sent to the Public Guardianship Office (formerly the Public Trust Office) on *Form EP2 Application for registration*. It is not acceptable to apply by letter. The completed form must be accompanied by the original EPA and a cheque for the registration fee made payable to 'The Public Guardianship Office'. The current fee is £220, although check with The Public Guardianship Office for any changes.

What if there is financial hardship?

Normally, no application will be considered if the registration fee has not been paid. However, it may be that the Attorney(s) is experiencing financial difficulties and cannot afford to pay the fee straightaway. If this is the case, the Attorney(s) should state this in a covering letter with the *Application*. The Public Trustee may allow the application to proceed in cases of genuine financial hardship, as long as payment is made as soon as money can be obtained from the Donor's funds.

When must the Application be made?

It must be made by first-class post within 10 days of the day on which the last of the notices to the Donor and the relatives was given. Send the *Application* to:

> The Public Guardianship Office Protection Division
> Stewart House
> 24 Kingsway
> London WC2B 6JX

Objections to the registration of the EPA

The Public Guardianship Office will not register the EPA immediately upon receipt of it. They will check through the papers and wait for a period of five weeks from the date of the last notification on a *Form EP1* before registering. Registration will take place after this time if no objections have been received during the five-week period.

Grounds on which objections may be raised

The grounds for objection are listed on the *Notice of intention to apply for registration* (*Form EP1*, page 171). Any objection which is not related to one of the five grounds will not be investigated by the Public Trustee. For example, relatives have no automatic right to be named as Attorney and cannot object that they are not one of the Attorneys named on the EPA.

A person wishing to object to the registration of a power must submit to the Court of Protection in writing his or her name and address, the Donor's name and address, the objector's relationship to the Donor, the Attorney's name and address, and the grounds of the objection. A copy of the objection may be supplied to the Attorney by the Public Guardianship Office and, if the disagreement cannot be sorted out between the Attorney and the objector, the Court of Protection may fix a date for a hearing. If the objection is upheld, the EPA will be cancelled and will not be registered. Otherwise, the EPA will be returned to the Attorney, stamped and sealed by the Court of Protection, and thus registered.

Cancellation of registration

Once the registration is complete, the Court will treat any objection as an application to cancel the registration. The Court may direct that an application to cancel registration be made on *Form EP3*. The Court can cancel a registration for the following reasons:

1. If it confirms the revocation of the power by the Donor, which must have been made when he or she was mentally capable, or receives notice of disclaimer by the Attorney.

2. If it gives a direction revoking the power upon exercising any of its powers under part VII of the Mental Health Act 1983.

3. If it is satisfied that the Donor is, and is likely to remain, mentally capable.

4. If it is satisfied that the power has expired or has been revoked by the death or bankruptcy of the Donor, the death, mental incapacity or bankruptcy of the Attorney or, if the Attorney is a corporation, upon its winding up or dissolution.

5. If it is satisfied that the power was not a valid and continuing enduring power when the registration was effected.

6. If it is satisfied that fraud or undue pressure was used to induce the Donor to create the power.

7. If it is satisfied that the Attorney's relationship to or connection with the Donor makes him or her unsuitable to be the Donor's Attorney.

The Court should always be notified of the death or recovery of the Donor.

Summary of the registration process

1. The Attorney(s) believe(s) that the Donor is, or is becoming, mentally incapable.

2. The Attorney(s) give(s) notice on *Form EP1* to at least three relatives in order of priority (see page 60) and the Donor in person, of their intention to register the EPA. All notices must be served within 14 days of each other.

3. Within 10 days of the date on which the last notice to the Donor or to relatives was given, the Attorney(s) must send the *Application for registration Form EP2*, together with the original EPA and the registration fee.

4. The Public Guardianship Office will inspect the paperwork and hold it for a period of five weeks from the date on which the last notice on a *Form EP1* was served. During this period, anyone may object to the registration.

5. If no objections are received and all the papers are in order, the EPA will be registered after the expiry of the five-week period.

6. If objections are received, they will be investigated, following which the EPA will either be revoked or cancelled or it will be registered.

Where can I get more information about registering EPAs?

Further enquiries about registering an EPA only may be made to:

General Enquiries
Public Guardianship Office
Archway Tower
2 Junction Road
London N19 5SZ

Telephone: 020 7664 7000
Email: custserv@guardianship.gov.uk

The Public Guardianship Office carries out administrative functions on behalf of the Court of Protection and does not give advice on actually making the Enduring Power of Attorney. You should consult a solicitor or Citizens Advice Bureau if you have questions about your legal rights and obligations, or need further assistance in preparing these forms.

For Scotland

Registering a CPA

The Attorney may apply to the Office of the Public Guardian for registration of the CPA at any time after the CPA is signed (whether the Donor is mentally capable or incapable).

After the CPA is signed and the Certificate completed, the application for registration must be completed (see example on page 183), including being signed by the Attorney confirming his or her agreement to act. The Public Guardian will refuse to register a CPA without confirmation from the Attorney (within the application for registration of the CPA) that he or she is willing to act as Attorney.

The application to register the CPA must be sent to The Office of the Public Guardian. It is not acceptable to apply by letter. The completed form must be accompanied by the original CPA with the appropriate Certificate and a cheque for the registration fee (currently £35), made payable to 'Scottish Court Services'.

The Public Guardian

Once the CPA is registered with the Public Guardian, the Attorney is responsible for intimating to the Public Guardian a change of address of the Attorney or of the Donor.

Should the Attorney die, his or her executor or representative must advise the Public Guardian; or of any other event which would terminate the CPA, for example, the Donor whilst still capable recalling the CPA.

The Public Guardian can investigate (a) complaints regarding the exercise of functions relating to the property or financial affairs of the Donor; or (b) any circumstances made known to him or her in which the property or financial affairs of the Donor seem to be at risk.

Where can I get more information about registering CPAs?

Codes of Practice

Section 13 of the Adults with Incapacity (Scotland) Act 2000 provides for the preparation of a Code of Practice containing guidance as to the exercise of the functions of a CPA. Copies of this Code can be obtained from:

> The Scottish Executive
> Justice Department
> Civil Law Division
> Saughton House
> Broomhouse Drive
> Edinburgh EH11 3XD

Further enquiries about registering a CPA may be made to:

> The Office of the Public Guardian
> Hadrian House
> Callendar Business Park
> Callendar Road
> Falkirk FK1 1XR
>
> Telephone: 01324 678300
> Fax: 01324 678301
> Email: opg@scotcourts.gov.uk

You should consult a Solicitor or Citizens Advice Bureau if you have any questions about your legal rights and obligations, or need further assistance in preparing a CPA.

Chapter 15: General Powers of Attorney

A General Power of Attorney (GPA) is, like an EPA, a form for authorising an Attorney to act on the Donor's behalf and in his or her name. But the important difference between an EPA and a GPA is that a GPA is automatically annulled in the event of the Donor becoming mentally incapable, whereas an EPA remains in force, subject to its registration. A GPA is a straightforward authorisation, without any complications.

A GPA is a useful means of creating a power of attorney for a specific period or event, when the age and health of the Donor make it unlikely that he or she could become mentally incapable during the duration of the power. The need for a GPA might arise, for example, when a person goes abroad for some time and wishes to entrust the management of business interests to a family member.

The rules governing who can be a Donor or an Attorney are the same as for an EPA, i.e. they must over 18, of full mental capacity and not an undischarged bankrupt.

Scope and restrictions

Once a General Power is granted the Attorney has full legal authority to take decisions and actions on the Donor's behalf, as if the Donor were taking them himself or herself, except that the Attorney cannot make gifts even to the limited extent which an EPA allows. Unlike an EPA, there is no provision in England and Wales for limiting the scope of the power in a General Power; but otherwise the extent and scope of the two are the same. This could be signing letters and cheques, or buying and selling property and shares (unless held in trust).

In Scotland as with a CPA, if the donor wishes to impose any limitations or restrictions (for example, for a specific or limited authority) that restriction should be clearly stated at the end. Ambiguous wording can undermine a GPA. A Donor may choose to appoint different Attorneys to deal with different parts of his or her property.

The GPA does not need endorsing or countersigning by a solicitor to be effective; once a GPA is granted the Attorney has full legal authority to take decisions and actions on the Donor's behalf as if the Donor were taking them himself or herself to the extent authorised by the GPA. These could be signing (with 'as Attorney for .....') letters and cheques – a bank will need a specimen signature; or buying and selling shares (unless held in trust), although the Attorney will need to produce the Power when required. In Scotland, a GPA may not be sufficient to enable the Attorney to deal with important transactions (such as borrowing money or selling land or other things of value) unless the particular type of transaction were specifically authorised.

As with an EPA, the Power does not cover functions of the Donor which relate to certain special personal responsibilities, for example, an Attorney cannot perform in the Donor's role as a trustee or executor of someone's estate. An Attorney cannot execute the Granter's Last Will & Testament, take action concerning the Donor's marriage or delegate his Power.

It is important to bear in mind that the Donor does remain liable for the actions of the Attorney. Clearly the extent of the Power is such that it should only be given to somebody the Donor trusts implicitly.

Duration

If the Donor becomes mentally incapable the GPA is automatically annulled. Otherwise, a General Power remains valid until it is revoked. Powers can be revoked orally, but to avoid misunderstanding it is wise to write 'cancelled' on the original form or simply tear it up and also to intimate the revocation to any third party who may have been advised by the GPA.

The GPA would also be revoked by the death or bankruptcy of the Donor or Attorney.

Completing your General Power

First, remember that there are different forms which are appropriate for England and Wales and for Scotland (see completed examples on pages 180 and 186-7).

You should insert the date on which the Power is to begin. This should be the same as the date it is signed.

The Donor should enter his or her full name and address. Only one Donor may make a GPA.

Enter the full name and address of the Attorney or Attorneys. As with an EPA, if you are appointing more than one Attorney they may be appointed 'jointly' or 'jointly and severally'. There is an explanation of these terms on page 46. Once you have decided how they are to act, delete as appropriate.

The Donor should sign the General Power in the presence of a witness who should also sign it and add his or her address and occupation. An Attorney cannot act as a witness. Once this is done the GPA is in force, until revoked.

Chapter 16:
What is a Living Will?

Note that a Living Will is for use in England and Wales but not in Scotland. For Scotland, see the chapter on Welfare Powers of Attorney.

A Living Will is an advance declaration of your wishes on medical treatments which you could be given in the future. Treatment could be for any illness you have now or which you develop, or for ill health as a result of any accident which you might suffer. It is a way of letting your doctors and family know what medical procedures you would not want to receive if, at a time the treatment could be given to you, you are unable to communicate your wishes to them yourself because of mental and/or physical incapacity.

It is important to realise that you can only use a Living Will to refuse certain treatments or procedures. It is not possible to request specific treatments or procedures. You can use your Living Will to say what quality of life and level of treatment you would consider acceptable if you became incapacitated by a terminal disease or if you were in a persistent vegetative state (an irreversible coma where you are only kept alive by artificial feeding mechanisms).

The Living Will can be a general statement of your wishes and/or it can direct your doctors and family on your wishes in relation to specific illnesses and their possible treatments. You can also appoint someone you trust – maybe a close friend or family member – with whom you would like doctors to consult about any medical procedures which could be administered to you. This person, who is referred to as a Health Care Proxy, would be aware of your views and would be able to communicate your wishes to medical staff (see pages 181-2 for completed example).

The difference between a Living Will and an ordinary Will

A Living Will is only concerned with medical treatment when you are still alive. You cannot use it to communicate your wishes on any matters normally dealt with by an ordinary Will or a Last Will & Testament. In other words, you cannot use it to determine who will inherit your property when you die, who will be your executors, or who will be guardians to your children.

The difference between a Living Will and an EPA

When you make an Enduring Power of Attorney, you can give your Attorney a general or limited power to conduct business, legal and financial transactions on your behalf. However, an Attorney is not permitted to make any decisions on health care matters. You therefore need to make a Living Will and appoint a Health Care Proxy if you want to delegate decisions on your future health care.

Are Living Wills valid and enforceable?

At present, there are no laws in England and Wales about Living Wills, although a Draft Bill to make Living Wills legal, written by the English Law Commission, is being considered by Parliament. The extent to which a Living Will will be considered enforceable at the moment depends on the way it is written and what it asks or directs doctors to do.

In Scotland, there are likewise no laws about Living Wills but see chapter 18 on Welfare Powers of Attorney.

Advance Directives

An informed and competent adult has the right to refuse medical procedures if he or she wants, unless the refusal harms others or conflicts with any law either at the time or in advance, except where there is a risk of contagion or if it is a matter of hygiene or comfort. This is what is known as an 'Advance Directive'. The British Medical Association supports the use of Advance Directives and says that 'an unambiguous and informed advance refusal is as valid as a contemporaneous decision'. Recent cases have supported the view that an advance refusal of treatment will be valid and enforceable if the following are complied with:

- you were mentally capable of making the decision to refuse medical treatment;

- you understood what the consequences of the refusal would be;

- the situation that has arisen is clearly of the type to which your refusal was meant to apply;

- the decision was your own and was not made under the influence of any other person.

Remember, the Advance Directives to which a Living Will gives effect only apply to refusals of certain treatments. An adult cannot demand that certain procedures are given to him or her and, similarly, cannot say in advance what should be given. A Living Will which states that certain procedures should be administered – for example, that a lethal injection should be given in the final stages of a terminal illness – will not be valid and enforceable.

Is there anything which cannot be refused in advance?

Yes, generally, you cannot refuse the essentials of good medical and nursing practice. This will include, for instance, basic hygiene measures. It will also extend to pain relief and management of distressing symptoms, such as vomiting. You can refuse in advance to be given food and drink in certain circumstances and you can refuse tube feeding. However, the British Medical Association Code on Advance Directives makes it clear that food and drink should be available for patients and offered to them (though not forced on them) at all times.

Advance Statements

You can make advance statements of your wishes on certain treatments under the section 'Additional Directions on Future Health Care' on the Living Will Form (see page 182). An Advance Statement differs from an Advance Directive in that doctors are not obliged to follow your wishes as expressed in a Statement, but they are obliged to observe your wishes in an Advance Directive. This is because Advance Directives deal with refusals of treatment and only categorical refusals of treatments will be binding. For example, you may want to state that you would not want to receive electric shock treatment; doctors will take account of this and will treat this directive with respect. However, if you state that you would want to receive a particular treatment for cancer (rather than refuse something), then your request would not be binding although it may have persuasive force on doctors.

Health Care Proxies

It is unlikely that a Health Care Proxy's decisions would have legal force. However, it is recognised that it is helpful for patients to nominate Proxies to express their wishes as it adds support to an Advance Statement or if an Advance Directive cannot be found in time.

Living Wills and euthanasia

An Advance Directive in a Living Will is not the same as euthanasia. Euthanasia and assisted suicides are not legal and you cannot write a Living Will directing doctors and relatives to act in this way. Anyone who helps you die or kill yourself is committing a criminal offence.

What are the benefits of making a Living Will?

Many people are concerned about what will happen to them if they become very ill and are unable to communicate their wishes to anyone. Many fear the loss of dignity and the significantly decreased quality of life which can result from degenerative health conditions. Medical technology has now advanced to such a degree that people can be kept alive even when they are brain dead.

Some people, after careful consideration and discussion with their doctors, decide that they do not want to receive treatments which would result in a meaningless and prolonged artificial existence. They have the benefit of recording their decisions and peace of mind through knowing that this will be communicated to the doctors. Opinions on how long a life can and should be prolonged have become increasingly subjective and it is increasingly acknowledged that people should be allowed to have a say in their future medical care.

> *Example: John has been lying in a nursing home bed for two and a half years. There is no evidence that he can hear, see, think or feel. John's breathing is controlled by a ventilator connected by a tracheotomy tube implanted in his throat. His nourishment and wastes are controlled by more tubes. His friends and family feel certain that he would not want to live this way, but, technically, John is alive.*

If you go into a hospital or a nursing home without specific written instructions, or appropriate notes of conversations with doctors having been made on your medical notes, the institution you enter will be legally bound to keep you alive by whatever means are deemed necessary and appropriate by the medical staff. With a Living Will, you express your rational views on the circumstances in which you would not want such attempts to keep you alive to continue. A Living Will which has been made when a patient is in good health is advantageous later on as it is good evidence of your true feelings.

Doctors are sometimes reluctant to honour the refusals by seriously ill patients because they cannot be certain the decision is rationally made.

Another advantage of a Living Will is that you can let your family know what you want. Many families do not want to accept that their loved one is not going to recover and therefore feel that they have to try any procedure which is available.

Remember that you can change your mind at any time about a prior written directive in a Living Will and consent to treatment which you had previously decided to refuse.

What else should I think about?

You should bear in mind that your views may change over time. Your views may also change if/when you become ill. You must remember that you can alter your directions at any stage if you want. Advances in medical treatments may also cause you to change your mind.

Should I discuss my Living Will with others?

You are not bound to consult anyone when drawing up your Living Will. However, a Living Will involves other people in carrying out the decisions you have made. It is therefore strongly advised that you do discuss your wishes with those close to you and with medical staff who treat you.

Your family

Your spouse, immediate family and perhaps religious adviser will be more likely to support your decision if you have fully discussed the issues with them in advance.

Your doctors

It is extremely important that you discuss your views with your doctor(s), not only when you make your Living Will but at regular intervals after you have done so, too. Your doctor(s) will be able to advise you on any new techniques or treatments which might become available and which might make you change your mind on certain statements made in your Living Will. Your doctor will want to make sure you are fully aware of the medical options available to you and that your Living Will expresses your true wishes. You will also want to be certain that your doctor will honour your requests and your Living Will should be included in your medical records. Some doctors have moral or ethical objections to Living Wills. It is very important that there is discussion so that your doctor can inform you of his or her views and make other doctors aware of yours. You may wish to change your doctor if this happens.

Your Health Care Proxy

The individual who will act for you as your Proxy should fully understand your wishes so he or she can make decisions which most closely coincide with the decisions you would have made had you been capable. This may become very important if you make a Living Will which, for example, does not mention a specific illness or situation which later affects you. If he or she is fully aware of how you would have viewed it, he or she can then give invaluable advice to the doctor(s).

Chapter 17:
Preparing and completing a Living Will

For England and Wales

As there are no laws governing Living Wills, there are no specific eligibility requirements. It is assumed that anyone who is 18 or older and who is mentally competent can prepare a Living Will. Being mentally competent in this context means that you understand what you are proposing in your Living Will, you can consider it and come to a rational decision and understand the effect that your decisions will have.

The British Medical Association recognises that children are also entitled to have their views taken into account, but their views will not be legally binding on doctors.

The form of your Living Will should be in writing and should be signed by you. Your signature should be witnessed. If you want to record a Living Will on cassette or video, do so only in addition to providing a clear written version.

What are my options and how are my wishes expressed in a Living Will?

A *Living Will Form* (see completed example on pages 181-2) has some general directives and statements about future health care and what you consider to be an acceptable quality of life. It is impossible to anticipate every consideration which might later become relevant to your future health care or to know what medical treatments might be necessary, effective or likely to be administered. However, if you wish to add certain specific directions – perhaps about existing health care conditions or forms of treatment – then there is space for you to do so.

Pregnancy

If you are a woman and it is possible that you might become pregnant at some point in the future, you should consider how you would feel about the directions or requests you have made in your Living Will if you were pregnant. It is likely that your Living Will will not be considered to be valid if you are pregnant, unless you leave specific instructions, as medical procedures may be administered to try to help the foetus.

How are Living Wills witnessed?

Your Living Will should be witnessed by a mentally competent adult. Your witness should not be someone who might be a beneficiary under your ordinary Will, or the spouse of a beneficiary.

Where should Living Wills be kept?

It is important that people are aware that you have a Living Will, as, if your family and doctors do not know of its existence, or are not sure if it still exists, medical procedures could be administered to you in good faith which you would not have wanted.

It is a good idea to have several copies of the signed and witnessed Living Will and leave them with your spouse, your family, perhaps a good friend and with your doctor and/or hospital notes. Some people decide to have a card in their wallet alerting anyone who may attend to them in an accident of the existence of a Living Will and where it may be found.

Revising a Living Will

It is important that you consider the terms of your Living Will at regular intervals so that you can be aware of the latest position and others can be aware that your views are current. You may like to add your signature and the date to the bottom of your Living Will when you have done so. There is no need to make a new Living Will every time. However, if you want to make any changes to your Living Will, you should re-do it. If there is a Living Will which has some amendments it may well look like you were not sure, or that it has been tampered with and so will not be valid. A *Living Will Form* has space at the end for you to show that you have reconsidered it and your views still stand.

Revoking your Living Will

You always have the right to revoke your Living Will. The easiest way of doing this is by tearing it up or writing 'revoked' or 'cancelled' on it clearly. Remember that, if you have made several copies of your Living Will and distributed them to various people, you should tear up those copies too and inform the individuals concerned in the change in your opinions.

A later Living Will will automatically revoke an earlier one. However, it is better not to rely on this so as to avoid confusion among your family and doctors.

Instructions for completing your Living Will

Personal details

You should fill in your name, address, date of birth, National Health Number and your doctor's details in the first section. Write clearly in dark ink or type the details.

Medical treatment you wish to refuse

This section allows you to make Advance Directives to refuse future medical treatments which would prolong your life or keep you alive by artificial means. You should read this book carefully and consult with your doctors before you fill in this section.

If, after consideration, you agree with the statements, you should put a tick in the boxes after the statements on the right hand side. If you do not agree with the statements, you should cross the statement out entirely to avoid confusion among your relatives and doctors.

You will see that there are a number of blank spaces which you need to fill in. For example, you might want two independent medical practitioners' opinions on your health and chances of recovery.

Medical treatment you wish to accept

If you want to accept treatment to manage pain or relieve distressing symptoms, then put a tick in the box after the statement. Otherwise, cross out the entire paragraph. Bear in mind that your doctors will be obliged to provide some degree of basic medical care anyway.

If you may become pregnant

You should consider what you would want to happen if you were pregnant. It is important to discuss this with your doctor if you are unsure. If you would not normally want to receive medical interventions, but would be prepared to accept them if you were pregnant, then you should tick the box at the end of the statement. Bear in mind that medical treatments may be administered to you anyway if the courts say so, in order to protect your unborn child.

Health Care Proxy

You should fill in the name and address of anybody you wish to appoint as your Proxy. Make sure you have discussed it fully with him or her first and he or she is willing to be named.

Additional directions on health care

You will see that there is a space for you to fill in any additional directions or wishes you may have. For example, you may already be suffering from a particular illness and have strong views about particular treatments which you can envisage being administered to you in the future. Some people may wish to request that a particular person, perhaps a family member or friend, be contacted to come to be with them if their death is imminent. You may wish to receive treatments temporarily to keep you alive until they arrive, if this is possible. You need to consider your options carefully.

Signatures

Once you have completed your *Living Will Form* and you are happy with what it says and the effects it will have, you should sign the form and add the date. You should sign in the presence of a witness, who should also sign and date the form (see page 182).

After you and the witness have signed the form, you should make copies of it and store it with the appropriate people.

Affirming your Living Will

At the end of the form is a space for signing the Living Will at some future date to show that you still have the same beliefs as set out in your Living Will. Remember to sign the form in the presence of a witness as above and add the date when you do so.

Chapter 18:
Welfare Powers of Attorney

For Scotland

In Scotland, a Welfare Power of Attorney (WPA) enables the Attorney to make decisions in regard to the welfare of the Donor when the Donor is incapable of doing so himself (but not otherwise). Such decisions might be in regard to medical treatment or the choice of where the Donor lives.

To be valid, a WPA must be granted by the Donor whilst he or she is mentally capable and must be registered with the Office of the Public Guardian in a manner similar to registration of a CPA.

Similar to a CPA, a WPA must include statements:

(i)   by the Donor to show that he or she intends the WPA to apply after subsequent mental incapacity;

(ii)   by the Donor to show that he or she has read or has had read to him or her the information explaining the effect of creating a WPA; and

(iii) in the registration application form by the Attorney to show that he or she is willing to act as Attorney under the WPA.

The WPA can be used only *after* the Donor is incapable of acting himself or herself notwithstanding that it will have been registered with the Office of the Public Guardian.

The Donor can revoke the WPA at any time after it has been registered as long as he or she is still mentally capable. If you would want to do that, you should consult a solicitor to draft a Deed of Revocation.

A WPA will be terminated (a) where the Donor and the Attorney are married to each other upon the granting of a Decree of Separation or divorce to either party or a declarator of nullity of marriage unless the WPA states otherwise; or (b) on the appointment of a guardian with powers related to those conferred in the WPA.

A WPA requires an accompanying Certificate in the prescribed form (slightly different from the Certificate which must accompany the CPA) which must be signed by a Prescribed Person who can be either a solicitor, a practising member of the Faculty of Advocates or a registered medical practitioner. The Certificate states that the Prescribed Person has interviewed the Donor immediately before the Donor subscribed the WPA and that he or she has satisfied himself or herself that at the time the WPA is granted, the Donor understands its nature and extent and that he or she has no reason to believe that the Donor is acting under undue influence or that any other factor prevents the granting of the WPA.

The person who signs the required WPA Certificate cannot be the Attorney.

After the WPA is signed and the Certificate completed the Application for Registration must be completed and signed by the Attorney confirming his or her agreement to act. The Public Guardian will refuse to register the WPA without confirmation from the Attorney (within the Application for Registration of the WPA) that he or she is willing to act.

The Application to Register the WPA must be sent to the Office of the Public Guardian. The completed form must be accompanied by the original WPA with Certificate and a cheque for the registration fee (currently £35) made payable to 'Scottish Court Services'.

Once the WPA is registered with the Public Guardian, the Attorney is responsible for intimating to the Public Guardian a change of address of the Attorney or of the Donor.

Should the Attorney die, the executor or representative must advise the Public Guardian; or of any other event (such as the Donor recalling the WPA) which would terminate the WPA.

Part 3

Probate

Chapter 19:
Probate and the administration of an estate: an overview

1. Register the death and obtain copies of the death certificate.

2. Attend to the funeral, burial, cremation, etc.

3. Find and review the deceased's Last Will & Testament.

4. Determine who the executors are and whether they are able and willing to act. If not, or if the deceased did not leave a valid Will, determine who will act as administrators of the estate. Get the agreement of the personal representatives in writing.

5. (a) In England and Wales, apply to the Personal Application Department of the most accessible and convenient Probate Registry for the forms required.

    (b) In Scotland, application for Confirmation (the Scottish equivalent of probate) is made to the Commissary Department of the Sheriff Court serving the area in which the deceased was domiciled at the time of death, which may be different from the place where the deceased died, for example, the death may have occurred in a hospital away from the area in which the deceased was domiciled. (**NB** If the deceased was domiciled outside Scotland or if the domicile is not known, then the application has to be made to the Commissary Office of the Sheriff Court in Edinburgh.) The required application forms for Confirmation can be obtained from the Sheriff Clerk concerned.

6. Secure the house and/or other property of the deceased, insuring the house, car and any other valuable items as necessary.

7. Organise yourself for valuing assets, corresponding with others, keeping financial records and receiving the deceased's mail. Open an executors' bank account.

8. Write to all financial and business organisations in which the deceased had an interest. Include a copy of the death certificate and request the necessary information for the probate or Confirmation application.

9. List the deceased's assets and liabilities. Review them. Is it necessary to apply for a grant of probate or Confirmation? If the estate appears to be insolvent or there are other complexities, see a solicitor.

10. If the estate appears to be worth more than £255,000 make arrangements to raise money, for example, by borrowing or selling some of the deceased's personal property, to pay inheritance tax before the grant of probate or Confirmation can be issued. Consider raising the funds from the deceased's own account using the Inheritance Tax Direct Payment Scheme (form *D20*).

11. Fill out probate or Confirmation forms as information is collected and return them to the Probate Registry or Sheriff Court concerned. In Scotland, the form of aplication for Confirmation is an *Inventory Form C1*. However, if the estate is neither a small estate nor an excepted estate (i.e. generally where the value of estate exceeds £240,000), then it is necessary for *Form IHT 200* to be completed and submitted to the Capital Taxes Office in Edinburgh prior to applying for Confirmation.

12. (a) In England and Wales, when the Probate Registry contacts the executors, all executors visit the Registry or local office to sign or swear the necessary forms and pay probate fees.

    (b) In Scotland, it is not necessary for the executors to attend at the Sheriff Court concerned as one of the executors can complete the necessary *Form C1* which is the application for Confirmation and mail it to the Sheriff Court concerned. If the deceased did not leave a Will, then normally it is necessary for a Bond of Caution (an insurance indemnity) to be obtained from an insurance company and lodged with the application for Confirmation. Such a Bond of Caution would not be required if there was a surviving spouse as the deceased's estate would pass to that spouse in terms of the Law of Intestate Succession in Scotland. (**NB** The premium for any required Bond of Caution is likely to be of the order of £300 or more depending on values and circumstances.)

13. Pay any inheritance tax due at the time of application and arrange for instalment payments if any of the assets qualify.

14. The Probate Registry or Sheriff Court concerned sends the grant of probate or Confirmation to you by post along with in England and Wales any additional probate copies (sealed copies) ordered or in Scotland Certificates of Confirmation. (**NB** In Scotland, a Certificate of Confirmation relates to one specific item of estate.)

15. Send copies of the grant of probate or the appropriate Certificate of Confirmation to each organisation contacted in Step 8 to show the executors' entitlement to deal with the deceased's assets. In return, organisations release the deceased's assets to the executors and close or transfer the deceased's accounts and files.

16. Advertise for creditors, if necessary. If any large or unexpected claims result, you should consider consulting a solicitor.

17. Respond to any queries raised by the Inland Revenue concerning the values of assets or liabilities of the estate. Agree final figures with them. Report any additional assets or liabilities that have come to light since probate or Confirmation was granted.

18. When all assets are collected, pay debts, including any unpaid income tax and capital gains tax relating to the deceased's income up to the time of death.

19. Ask the Inspector of Taxes for an income tax return and complete it with details of the income of the estate to the end of the tax year during which the deceased died. Pay any tax due. A return may also be needed for each subsequent tax year if the administration of the estate is not complete within one tax year.

20. Ask the Inland Revenue's Capital Taxes Office for *Form IHT 30* (*Application for formal discharge from inheritance tax*); complete it and have it signed by all the executors and in due course receive the signed discharge certificate from the Revenue.

21. Check that there have been no claims against the estate (in England or Wales under the Inheritance (Provision for Family and Dependants) Act 1975) during the six months following the grant of probate or Confirmation. Barring any such challenges, the estate can be distributed.

22. When all the assets have been accounted for and debts paid, legacies can be distributed. Get a receipt from each beneficiary.

23. When all cheques have cleared, close the executors' account.

24. Draw up estate accounts. Get approval of the accounts from all residuary beneficiaries (or those entitled under the intestacy laws)

and send them copies. Issue *Inland Revenue Form R185 (Estate Income)* to the residuary beneficiaries showing their shares of the income of the estate and the tax deducted from it during the tax year.

25. The administration of the estate is now complete. All accounts should be saved for 12 years.

Chapter 20:
What is an executor?

When someone is named the executor of a Will, he or she is being asked to take responsibility for administering the estate of the person who made the Will, called the testator, upon the testator's death. Acting as an executor should not be undertaken lightly. Immediately following the death the executors are expected to begin their administrative duties; long after other mourners' lives have returned to normal, the executors will still be administering the estate. This entails corresponding with other parties, keeping meticulous records, filling out forms and being answerable to creditors, beneficiaries and the intentions of the deceased, as recorded in the Will.

Do not be put off by the term 'estate'. This simply refers to all the property a person leaves behind, whether its value be hundreds or millions of pounds. One person's assets may include homes, yachts and a Swiss bank account, whilst another leaves a wedding ring, some changes of clothes and a shoe-box full of costume jewellery. Both have left estates to be accounted for and distributed.

Executors' duties can be summed up as: taking an inventory of the deceased's possessions and debts, collecting the assets, paying the bills and distributing the legacies (whether specific items, cash sums or residue) following the testator's wishes as closely as possible. The following chapters take you through the probate process in England and Wales or the Confirmation process in Scotland, without the services of a solicitor.

Grant of probate or Confirmation

Executors have the power to deal with the deceased's assets from the date of death, but not until they receive what is called in England and Wales, a grant of probate or in Scotland, Confirmation, can they prove their authority to those institutions and authorities that hold assets in the deceased's name. In England and Wales, grants of probate are issued by the High Court through Probate Registries. In Scotland, Confirmation is issued by the Commissary Department of the Sheriff Court in the area where the deceased had been domiciled at death (see chapter 26).

More than one executor

If the Will appoints only one executor, or if only one person is able and willing to act, a grant of probate or Confirmation can be issued to one person. If the Will appoints more than four executors, only four of them will be allowed to apply for the grant of probate or Confirmation. The others may renounce their right to apply for probate or Confirmation. Or they may decide not to apply for the time being but to reserve their right to apply in the future so that if, for example, one of the acting executors dies before the estate has been fully administered, the executor with power reserved may take his or her place.

In England and Wales, if only one executor is taking out the grant of probate, it may be prudent for the other executor(s) to sign what's called a power reserved letter, even if it is not anticipated that he or she will want to apply at any stage. By reserving the right to apply in this way, a non-acting executor can step in if the acting executor becomes incapacitated before the administration of the estate is complete. The Probate Registry (see chapter 26 for contact addresses) provides a form necessary to renounce or reserve the right to apply for probate. In Scotland, Confirmation is always issued in favour of all executors who have been nominated and who have not declined office.

No matter how many executors are named, for practical purposes it is usually easier if one of the executors undertakes the administrative tasks on behalf of them all (he or she is referred to in this book as the first applicant). The executors should meet to discuss the practical side of carrying out their duties. Whatever is agreed should be put in writing and signed by them all. In fact, all official paperwork may need to be signed by all executors, even if they agree that one of them is the first applicant (the exception being that in Scotland the application for Confirmation (*C1 Account*) requires to be signed by only one executor).

Caution: If it looks as though the deceased's estate is insolvent, i.e. the debts of the deceased and other liabilities of the estate, including funeral expenses, will exceed the value of the assets in the estate, executors should think carefully before applying for the grant of probate or Confirmation. If the estate may be insolvent, it is prudent to seek the advice of a solicitor before taking any further steps.

Other personal representatives

If an executor renounces the right to take out the grant of probate or in Scotland if a nominated executor declines to accept office, any substitute executor named in the Will steps in and proceeds to apply for the grant of probate or Confirmation. If no executor is named in the Will or if the executor named cannot or does not wish to act and no substitute is named, beneficiaries can apply to act as the deceased's *personal representatives*. A beneficiary acting as the testator's personal representative is, in England and Wales, known as the *administrator* and the grant itself is called a *grant of letters of administration with Will annexed*. An administrator's duties are essentially the same as those of an executor. This book refers to executors, but the rights and responsibilities of both are the same in most respects, whether the person doing the work is an executor or an administrator.

In England and Wales, beneficiaries may apply for a grant as the deceased's administrators in the following order of priority:

1. any residuary legatee;

2. any personal representative of a residuary legatee;

3. any other legatee;

4. any personal representative of any other legatee;

5. any creditor.

In Scotland, an executor appointed in terms of a Will is called an *executor-nominate* and an executor appointed by the Court is called an *executor-dative*. Where there is no Will (or in some cases where there is a Will but where there is no surviving executor who agrees to accept office or where there is no other person entitled to be appointed executor-nominate) the order of priority to be appointed executor-dative is:

1. a general disponee universal legatory or residuary legatee;

2. any one of the next of kin or heirs on intestacy (if there is a surviving spouse he or she would normally be preferred and would be exclusively entitled where the value of the deceased's estate is less than the spouse's prior rights);

3. creditors;

4. specific legatees.

An executor-dative is appointed on application to the Sheriff Court in the area where the deceased had been domiciled at the date of his death. That application is by way of Petition in prescribed form. The Sheriff Clerk's Office may assist you in preparing the required Petition. The fee to accompany such Petition is £11 (at present).

A minor (someone under the age of 18) may not act as an executor. In England and Wales, if a minor is the only executor appointed in a Will, his or her parents or guardian are entitled to take out a grant of letters of administration with Will annexed on his or her behalf. The minor has the right to apply for the grant of probate on attaining his or her 18th birthday, if the administration of the estate has not been completed.

If the deceased left no Will, he or she is said to have died *intestate* and the estate is distributed in accordance with the rules of intestacy. In England and Wales, the personal representatives are, again, known as administrators and the grant is called a *grant of letters of administration*. In Scotland, the personal representatives are when appointed known as executors-dative but the grant is still known as Confirmation. In England and Wales, when there is no Will administrators are appointed in the following order of priority:

1. the deceased's spouse;

2. any child of the deceased and any issue of a child who died before the deceased;

3. the parents of the deceased;

4. brothers and sisters of the whole blood of the deceased and the issue of any who died before the deceased;

5. brothers and sisters of the half blood of the deceased and the issue of any who died before the deceased;

6. grandparents of the deceased;

7. uncles and aunts of the whole blood and the issue of any who died before the deceased;

8. uncles and aunts of the half blood and the issue of any who died before the deceased.

In England and Wales, the maximum number of administrators is four, whether there is a Will or the person died intestate. A sole administrator may take out the grant only where none of the beneficiaries is under 18 or where no *life interest* arises. If either of these is the case, the grant must issue to a minimum of two administrators.

In England and Wales, a life interest most commonly arises where the deceased's estate is worth more than £125,000 and he or she died intestate leaving a spouse and a child or children. In that case, the spouse will take the first £125,000 as a legacy, all the personal chattels, and will have a life interest in half of the residue of the estate: the remaining half of the estate is held in trust for the child or children until reaching 18; they also benefit from the spouse's life interest on his/her death.

In Scotland, in an intestate estate no 'liferent' (or life interest) arises and the beneficiaries in intestacy are explained elsewhere.

Should a solicitor be instructed?

Executors can instruct a solicitor, stockbroker or other adviser to perform specific duties even if they do not use a solicitor to make the probate or Confirmation application. Whether an executor handles all the tasks involved in administering the estate or uses professional advisers is a matter of choice and convenience. Any fees properly incurred are paid out of the estate.

This book is designed to help the layperson sort out a simple, straightforward Will or intestacy. If the Will or the estate is complex, a solicitor should be consulted. If you are in any doubt, seek professional advice. Some signs that a solicitor should be involved include the following:

1. the estate is insolvent;

2. a beneficiary cannot be contacted;

3. someone intends to challenge the Will;

4. there is some question of the Will's validity, or the Will cannot be found;

5. someone stands to inherit a life interest in, or liferent of, the estate;

6. beneficiaries include children under the age of 18 and a trust is set up for them;

7. the deceased owned a business or was a partner in a business;

8. the deceased was a Name (i.e. investor) in Lloyd's of London insurance market;

9. a trust is set up under the Will;

10. any house or land in the estate has an unregistered title.

Chapter 21:
When death occurs

When someone dies a doctor should be called. He or she will issue a medical certificate stating the cause or causes of death, along with a notice setting out who is eligible to register the death with the local Registrar of Births and Deaths.

Registering the death

In England and Wales, if the death has occurred inside a house or public building, the following people may act as informant, in the following order:

1. a relative of the deceased who was present at the death;

2. a relative of the deceased who was present during the final stages of the illness;

3. a relative of the deceased who lives in the district where the death occurred;

4. anyone who was present at the death;

5. someone in authority in the building where the death occurred who was aware of the circumstances of the death, for example, the owner of a nursing home or the warden of sheltered accommodation;

6. any resident of the building where the death occurred, if he or she was aware of the circumstances of the death;

7. the person who accepts responsibility for arranging the funeral.

If the death occurred outside a house or public building, the following people are eligible to register the death in the following order:

1. a relative of the deceased able to provide the Registrar with the necessary details;

2. anyone who was present at the death;

3. the person who found the body;

4. the person in charge of the body (the police if the body is unidentified);

5. the person who accepts responsibility for arranging the funeral.

In Scotland, the death must be registered by:

1. any relative of the deceased;

2. any person present at the death;

3. the executor or other legal representative of the deceased;

4. the occupier at the time of death of the premises where the death occurred;

5. if there is no person as above, any other person having knowledge of the particulars to be registered.

In England and Wales, within five days, or in Scotland within eight days, of the death, the informant must take the medical certificate to the Registrar of Deaths, or must send written notice. In England and Wales, the deceased's medical card should be given to the Registrar as well. The Registrar will ask for other details about the deceased:

1. the date and place of death (birth certificate should be produced if available);

2. the full name of the deceased, including any maiden name;

3. the date and place of birth of the deceased;

4. the occupation of the deceased;

5. the name, date of birth and occupation of the deceased's spouse (and in Scotland, former spouses), whether or not still living;

6. the deceased's usual address;

7. whether the deceased received any state pension or allowance;

8. the date of birth of any surviving spouse;

9. in Scotland, the full names and occupations of the parents of the deceased should also be provided (if known).

The death certificate

Once the death has been registered, the informant will be given a death certificate, which is a copy of the entry on the register (and in Scotland, also a certificate for the Funeral Director dealing with the funeral). There is a small charge for each copy, and it is sensible to get three or four copies. The executors may need to send copies to the deceased's bank, to the registrars of companies in which he or she held shares, to insurance companies holding policies written in trust and, in England and Wales, to the Probate Registry. Although you can have the certificate returned to you once it has been inspected, it may be more convenient to circulate several copies at once.

Note: A while after the death the cost of a copy of the death certificate may increase. The period varies depending on the register office so it is worth checking if it is probable further copies will be needed.

The Will

If the executors are prepared for their duties, they may have been in possession of a copy of the Will even before the death and know the location of the original. They may know of the deceased's instructions concerning organ donation, disposal of the body and funeral wishes. All of this information is needed in the first hours following death.

Arranging the funeral is not specifically the duty of executors and should be handled by whoever is most aware of the deceased's wishes. But anyone who manages the funeral is entitled to have the account settled out of money from the estate.

If there is no opportunity for preparation before the death the Will must be located to determine who has been named its executor(s). If no Will is found at the deceased's home, it may have been sent to his or her bank or solicitor for safekeeping. In England and Wales, it may have been deposited at the Principal Registry (formerly Somerset House), in which case a deposit certificate will have been issued on receipt of the Will; the Will can be reclaimed by sending the certificate to:

> The Principal Registry
> Family Division, Safe Custody Department
> First Avenue House
> 42–49 High Holborn
> London WC1V 2NP

If a Will is found, ascertain that it is the deceased's last Will by making enquiries at the deceased's bank and solicitor, for example. It must bear the signature of the deceased and of an appropriate witness or witnesses. In England and Wales, probate may be granted on a copy, but you should notify the Probate Registry as soon as possible that the original cannot be found. The Registry will tell you what evidence is needed as proof that the original Will had not been revoked by being destroyed before death.

The necessity of a formal 'reading of the Will' before hopeful beneficiaries, or a solicitor, is a myth. There is no legal requirement for any such reading but it is courteous to write to beneficiaries to inform them of their entitlement under the Will (in Scotland, this is very often done only after Confirmation is issued in favour of the executors).

There may be some doubt as to who the beneficiaries are under the Will. Many Wills describe certain beneficiaries in terms of groups of people, for example 'my children,' rather than naming them. The expression 'my children' includes, by law, children conceived at the time of the deceased's death and subsequently born alive, adopted children and, in England and Wales, legitimated children (children born to unmarried parents who later marry). In Scotland, illegitimate children (i.e. children born outside marriage) are also included in the expression 'my children'.

If the Will was executed after 3rd April 1988, children whose parents were married to each other at the time of their birth are treated in the same way as those whose parents were not, even if the executors have no knowledge of the children's existence. In England and Wales, if the Will was executed before then, the executors will not be liable to a testator's child born outside marriage if they did not know of his or her existence. These rules apply unless it is clear from the Will that the deceased intended otherwise.

Generally, if a beneficiary named in a Will has died before the testator, the gift to him or her will simply not take effect. However, if that beneficiary is a child, grandchild or great-grandchild of the testator (or in Scotland, a close relative, such as nephew or niece of the testator), and he or she has left children of his or her own, the children step into or may step into their parent's shoes and their entitlement under the Will, shared equally between them.

In England and Wales (but *not* in Scotland), if the deceased married after making the Will and the Will was not expressed to be in expectation of the marriage, the Will is automatically revoked. Divorce, however, does not revoke a Will, but in England and Wales (but *not* in Scotland), the former spouse is treated as if he or she died on the date of the divorce so that he or she cannot take a gift under the Will or act as an executor.

If the executors are uncertain as to the interpretation of other parts of the Will, they should seek the advice of a solicitor to avoid the risk of distributing the money wrongly.

Once probate or Confirmation is granted the Will becomes a public document, but until then the beneficiaries may know nothing of their legacies, unless the deceased told them before he or she died. However, the executors will usually tell the beneficiaries that they have been left a legacy although it is impossible to be specific about the amount if it is a legacy of residue or part of residue. (In Scotland, this is very often done only after Confirmation is issued in favour of the executors.) But no legacy can be guaranteed at this stage as the Will may be found invalid, may be challenged, or the assets of the estate may not be sufficient to pay all the legacies.

Chapter 22:
Duties of an executor

In preparation for dealing with the assets and liabilities of the estate, some administrative tasks should be attended to by the executors as soon as possible.

Have the deceased's postal address changed to that of the first applicant, the executor who is to handle day-to-day business and personal affairs. If the home is to be left unoccupied the executors should ensure that it is securely locked; that water, electricity and gas supplies have been turned off and mail re-directed.

The executors should also ensure that there are both current buildings and contents insurance policies on the home. The executors may be held liable by any beneficiary who receives less from the estate than he or she should because of a burglary, fire or other loss. The insurers should be notified of the death and given the names and addresses of the executors. If there are particularly valuable items at the deceased's home and it is to be left unoccupied, it may be better to remove them for safekeeping.

Finally, the executors should open an executors' bank account into which they will eventually deposit the proceeds of assets and from which they will pay the bills of the deceased.

Make a thorough search of the deceased's papers for the documents that will be needed to finalise the deceased's affairs. These will include:

- cheque books;

- bank statements;

- savings certificates and other national savings assets;

- outstanding bills;

- share certificates and stockbroker's details;

- car registration documents;

- mortgage papers;

- insurance and pension documentation;

- information on jewellery and collectibles, for example, insurance valuations;

- tax assessments, returns and other tax papers.

The executor's aims are to:

1. identify the assets of the estate and assess their value at date of death;

2. identify the deceased's debts and pay them;

3. distribute the legacies.

Is a grant of probate or Confirmation necessary?

Whilst itemising the assets of the estate, the executors must bear in mind that it may not be necessary to apply for a grant of probate (England and Wales) or for Confirmation (Scotland). Whether or not a grant is required depends not only on the size of the deceased's estate, but also on the kinds of assets in it. Normally, a grant is required where the value of the deceased's estate (after paying the funeral account) exceeds £5,000. The grant vests authority in the executors to deal with the estate. Without that authority, the executors would be relying solely on the validity of the Will.

For example, if the deceased only left a great deal of cash, personal items having a high market value and a very expensive car, there is no need to apply for a grant of probate or Confirmation because executors need no formal proof of their authority to gather in and distribute such assets. On the other hand, if the deceased had a bank account and shares with a net value of over £5,000, or if the deceased's home needs to be sold or transferred to a beneficiary, a grant will be necessary so the executors can obtain formal authority to gather in and deal with these assets.

Certain authorities can pay sums due on death to the person entitled under a Will or intestacy without requiring sight of a grant of probate, as long as the amount payable is (normally) less than £5,000. The assets concerned include:

- **National Savings, including prizes won on Premium Bonds.** In order to claim, the executors need to complete *Form NSA 904*, which is available from post offices, and send it to the address given on that form for the type of account held, together with a registrar's copy of the death certificate.

- **Building society accounts, deposits with friendly societies, trade union deposits of members, arrears of salary or pension due to government or local government employees**

and police and firemen's pensions. The executors should write to the relevant authority, asking for a claim form and sending a registrar's copy of the death certificate.

Other assets that may be realised without the executors needing to produce the grant of probate or Confirmation are:

- **Nominated property.** Until 1981, the holder of certain National Savings investments and government stock could nominate someone to receive them on his death. After 1981, no new nominations could be made, but those made before that year are valid. Such a nomination takes effect independently of the deceased's Will or intestacy and independently of any grant of probate. The person nominated can have such stocks transferred into his or her name or redeemed on producing the death certificate. There is no upper limit on the value of the nominated property which can be dealt with in this way, but if the institution is concerned that the estate may be large enough for inheritance tax to be paid on it, it may require the executors to obtain a certificate from the Inland Revenue to show that any such tax has been paid.

- **Jointly held assets.** When two people hold property jointly (as joint tenants in England and Wales, or in Scotland where there is a specific or implied survivorship destination), on the death of one of them, his or her share of the asset passes directly to the other by right of survivorship, regardless of the provisions of the Will or the intestacy rules. Such assets might include a house or flat, or bank or building society accounts. No grant of probate or Confirmation is required to transfer the deceased's share of these assets to the surviving joint holder. If the property is a house or flat, and in England and Wales the land is registered land, a registrar's copy of the death certificate should be sent to the Land Registry to enable the survivor to be registered as the sole surviving owner of the house or flat. In England and Wales, if the land is unregistered land, a registrar's copy of the death certificate should be kept with the title deeds and will need to be produced when the land is sold. In Scotland, in regard to such property where there is a survivorship destination, no action is required (whether or not the property is registered in the Land Registry of Scotland) except that a copy of the death certificate should be held as part of the surviving owner's title. If the joint asset is a bank or building society account, a registrar's copy of the death certificate should be sent to the relevant bank or building society so the deceased's name may be removed from the account.

Therefore, if the deceased's estate consists solely of jointly held assets, there would normally be no need for the executors to apply for a grant of probate or Confirmation.

Probate or Confirmation forms

In England and Wales, the Probate Registry will supply the executors with the required forms, but it is best to ask for them early on in the probate process. In Scotland, the Sheriff Clerk's Office of the Sheriff Court in the area where the deceased had been domiciled at death will supply the executors with the required forms (see chapter 26 for contact addresses). As the inventory and valuation process progresses, executors can fill in the forms as they go along. Probate or Confirmation forms are discussed in more detail in chapter 24.

A note on Probate Registries in England and Wales: all executors will need to make at least one visit to the Probate Registry or a local office (*not* so in Scotland). In dealing with an estate in England and Wales, apart from the Principal Registry in London, there are district Registries and local offices under their control throughout the country (see chapter 26). It is sensible to choose a Registry or local office conveniently located for the executors; bear in mind that some local offices do have minimal and sporadic office hours which may not necessarily result in a quick or convenient service, and that not all Probate Registries have identical procedures.

Financial records

During the administration of the estate, the executors must keep track of every financial transaction, no matter how small. The money and assets belonging to the estate must be kept entirely separate from the executors' personal money and assets. Out-of-pocket expenses of the executors should be recorded as carefully as the payment of bank and probate fees or Confirmation dues or inheritance taxes.

Although executors are paid for their efforts only if the Will so specifies, expenses the executors incur such as postage, travel costs, telephone bills, etc., can be paid from the estate.

More importantly, the executors must be able to account for every penny of the testator's estate. They have a fiduciary responsibility (i.e. one of trust) to the creditors and beneficiaries of the estate. When the estate has been fully administered, the executors will need to draw up accounts to demonstrate to the beneficiaries how the assets of the estate were spent or distributed. Spotless, unimpeachable financial records are the executors' proof of what has occurred within the testator's estate, from the date of death to the date of the final distribution of assets.

Paying inheritance tax

Once a thorough valuation of the deceased's assets and liabilities is completed, any inheritance tax due must be paid *before* applying for the grant of probate or Confirmation. However, few financial institutions will hand over the funds of the deceased until there is a grant of probate or Confirmation to prove the executors' authority.

If the deceased had funds in a National Savings account or held National Savings Certificates and Premium Bonds, National Savings may issue a cheque in favour of the Inland Revenue to cover all or part of the tax, thereby permitting the grant of probate or Confirmation. Similar arrangements may be made between a building society account and the Inland Revenue. Other banks may be willing to arrange a loan to the executors to pay the inheritance tax, thereby releasing the funds to repay the loan. Further details are provided in chapter 23.

As an alternative to the above, it may be possible to arrange for the tax to be paid direct from the account in the deceased's sole name in a bank or building society, using Inland Revenue form D20. You will need to obtain a tax reference from the Capital Taxes Office (CTO) for the estate. When you are ready to apply for probare, send the D20 to the bank or building society and they will pay the CTO direct from the account.

Identifying beneficiaries

Once the liabilities of the estate have been paid, the executors identify the beneficiaries of the estate: either those named in the Will or those entitled under the intestacy rules. If the executors distribute the estate incorrectly, they are personally liable to the rightful beneficiaries and to creditors about whom they know or should have known.

In England and Wales, to protect themselves from unknown creditors and beneficiaries, the executors can follow a statutory procedure which involves the placing of advertisements for creditors in the *London Gazette* at:

> The London Gazette
> PO Box 7923
> London SW8 5WF
> Telephone: 020 7394 4580

They must also advertise in a newspaper circulating in the area where the deceased lived and, particularly if he or she owned a business, the area where he or she worked at the time of death. If land is to be distributed, an advertisement should also be placed in a newspaper circulating in the district where the land is situated.

The advertisements should state that anyone with a claim against or an interest in the estate must make their claim known within a stated time (not less than two months) from the date of the notice, after which the executors may distribute the estate, having regard only to those claims of which they have notice. After the stated time, in England and Wales, anyone who has not come forward cannot make a claim against the executors, although they may claim against the beneficiaries of the estate into whose hands assets have passed.

Advertising for unknown creditors may not be necessary if there is no reason to suspect that the deceased has incurred debts other than those known to the executor.

Note: Unlike an executor, an administrator in England and Wales can place statutory advertisements only after the grant of letters of administration has been issued.

Chapter 23: Taking stock

As a first step, the executors should list those assets which they know, based on personal observation or findings, the deceased owned. This chapter includes a checklist beginning on page 108 which sets out the most commonly owned assets.

Following this inventory by observation, the executor sends notification of the death to the deceased's bank, building society, accountant, insurance company and other institutions. The letters to the bank and building society should request information about each account and instruct them to stop all unpaid cheques and standing orders. Also ask for a list of deeds and other documents held on behalf of the deceased, for example, life policies, as at the date of death. Executors do not have to wait to receive the grant of probate or Confirmation to begin this notification and inventory, but a copy must be sent to each institution when it is received from (in England and Wales) the Probate Registry or (in Scotland) the Commissary Department of the Sheriff Court concerned. For the initial correspondence, it is sufficient to enclose a copy of the death certificate.

The goal is to get in writing the value of all the assets and debts as at the time of death. This information must be provided on the probate or Confirmation forms. Even if an asset is left as a legacy to a beneficiary, it must be listed and accounted for in the inventory.

Valuing debts

The following is a checklist of debts the deceased might owe. Information on any of these liabilities that apply should be included in section F of Inland Revenue *Form IHT 200*. This is the return of the testator's whole estate for inheritance tax purposes (see page 213 for completed example). If necessary, it is generally possible to request a delay in payment of debts until the grant has been obtained and funds are available.

1. water rates
2. telephone bill
} ask for a bill to the date of death;

3. electricity bill ⎫
⎬ take a meter reading on the date of death,
or as soon afterwards as possible and ask

4. gas bill ⎭ for a bill to that date;

5. loan or overdraft ⎱ write to the bank for the outstanding
⎰ balance;

6. credit card bills ⎫
write to the credit card company
⎬ asking for the amount of any
outstanding balance;
⎭

7. mail-order ⎫
catalogue bill write to notify the company on the death
⎬ and to ask whether any outstanding
balance is due;
⎭

8. rent arrears;

9. hire purchase payments;

10. debts owed by the deceased to other individuals;

11. outstanding income tax and capital gains tax.

Reasonable funeral expenses are also counted as a liability of the estate, including the cost of a grave-stone; these should be included in section F of Inland Revenue *Form IHT 200*. If the person arranging the funeral is in receipt of Income Support, Working Family Tax Credit or Housing Benefit, he or she may be able to apply to the Social Fund (a loan-type scheme administered by the Benefits Agency) for a payment to cover reasonable funeral expenses. However, the cost is repaid out of the estate if money subsequently becomes available.

Asset checklist

To help the executors make an inventory of assets, the following checklist itemises some of the typical ones found in an estate. As you go through it, refer to the completed examples of forms (beginning on page 196) which must be filed in England and Wales with the Probate Registry, or in Scotland with the Commissary Department of the Sheriff Court concerned. Not all the assets listed here are specifically categorised on *Form IHT 200*; those not listed should be recorded on *Supplementary page D17* and their total value included in F23 of *Form IHT 200* (see page 213 for completed example). Generally, the value reported for probate or Confirmation purposes should be the price an asset would fetch if sold on the open market on the date of death.

House or flat

If the deceased owned his or her own home jointly with another person, only the deceased's share of the home is treated as part of his or her estate. It will usually be a half-share unless the owners held the property as beneficial tenants in common or in some other specific proportions and the title deeds specify that they hold it in unequal shares. If two or more joint owners hold a property in England and Wales as beneficial tenants in common, or in Scotland without a survivorship destination, each person can leave his or her own share of the property to whomsoever he or she wishes under his or her Will. However, if they hold the property in England and Wales as beneficial joint tenants or in Scotland where there is a survivorship destination the share of a person who dies automatically passes to the survivor or survivors.

If the precise value is not relevant for calculating the inheritance tax due on the estate, for example, because the property or the deceased's share of it is to go to the deceased's spouse, an approximate value will normally be acceptable (see page 127). The executor should, however, ascertain as accurate an estimate of value as is reasonably practicable albeit that he or she may estimate the value himself or herself, by reference to the prices which similar properties in the area are fetching, or ask an estate agent for an informal valuation.

In some circumstances, it is better to ask an estate agent to make a formal valuation, for which a fee may be charged. For instance, if the property is to be transferred to a beneficiary as part of a legacy instead of cash, then the executor should have a formal valuation to ensure that the distribution among the beneficiaries is fair.

Whichever method is used, the value given will be checked by the District Valuer for the Inland Revenue, who may challenge it if it appears to be too low. If the property is sold soon after the death (although the executors will not be able to complete the sale until they have the grant showing their entitlement to deal with the property), the District Valuer would normally seek to substitute the sale price for the value submitted in the probate or Confirmation application. Details of the property should be included on *Supplementary page D12, Land, Buildings and Interest in Land* (see completed example on page 233).

If there is a mortgage on the deceased's house or flat, the mortgage lender should be notified. You should give the deceased's name, address and mortgage account number and enclose a copy of the death certificate. An example letter to a deceased's mortgage lender is provided on page 145. You will need to know how much of the mortgage was outstanding at the date of death, and whether there is a life assurance or mortgage protection policy linked to the mortgage. If there is, you should ask whether the cover is sufficient to repay the mortgage and whether there will be any surplus remaining after repayment.

Bank account

The executors must write to the deceased's bank and, if there is also a building society account, to the building society, with a registrar's copy of the death certificate, to inform them of the death and to instruct them to stop all unpaid cheques and standing orders. You should also ask for a list of all deeds, share certificates and other documents held on the deceased's behalf and the balances on the deceased's accounts at the date of death, with a separate figure for interest which had been earned on the money to that date, but not credited to the account. This information is needed for *Form IHT 200*. It is also useful to ask, in the same letter, what interest has been credited to the deceased's account during the tax year in which he or she died and whether it was paid net of tax or gross. This information will be needed for the tax return to the date of death. An example of a letter to a deceased's bank is provided on page 146.

The executors will also need to open a bank account in their own names to enable them to pay in cheques for the proceeds of sales of assets of the estate, and to write cheques to discharge liabilities. The executors' full names and addresses should be given to the bank, which will send a mandate for completion and signature by the executors.

Any cheques which are made payable to the deceased but which were not paid into his or her account before the death may be able to be paid into his or her account or the executors' account but the bank may insist that such cheques be endorsed in favour of the executors. Once a copy of the grant of probate or Confirmation has been shown to the bank, the bank can transfer the balance on the deceased's account to the executors' account.

Stocks and shares

If the deceased owned any shares, the certificates may be at the deceased's home or with his or her bank, solicitor or stockbroker. If they are at the home and it is to be left unoccupied, it is best to remove them for safe-keeping. It may be desirable to check with the registrar of each of the companies in which the shares were held to make sure that the holdings evidenced by the certificates are correct. The name and address of the registrar can usually be found on the counterfoil of the share certificate or you can look them up in the *Register of Registrars*, a publication which can be found in most reference libraries.

Sometimes, shareholdings are in the nominee name of the shareholder's stockbroker and the stockbroker will have the share certificates. If that is the case, there is no need to write to each of the company registrars, but the stockbroker should be notified of the death and sent a copy of the death certificate.

If any share certificates cannot be found, the executors may need to sign a statutory declaration and indemnity before selling them or transferring them to a beneficiary, for which the registrar of the company will charge a fee. It states that the executors have searched for the certificate and believe it to be lost, and the executors indemnify the company against any loss if the certificate comes to light later in the hands of a person who has a better claim to ownership of the shares than the executors do. Some shareholdings may be uncertificated and therefore no certificates are involved.

Once a complete list of shareholdings has been compiled, the executors can ask a stockbroker for a probate or Confirmation valuation, for which he or she will charge a fee, generally a fixed sum per holding. Alternatively, executors may make their own valuation by referring to the *Stock Exchange Daily Official List* for the day the deceased died. The *List* is available at public libraries or it can be bought from the Publications Section of the Stock Exchange in London.

For probate or Confirmation purposes the value of a stock is the lower of the two values quoted, plus a quarter of the difference between those values, for example, for a share quoted at 96–98p for that day, 96.5p would be the probate or Confirmation value.

If any of the shares are quoted 'XD' there is a dividend due to the deceased that has not yet been paid. If you are obtaining a valuation from a broker, he or she will include such dividends in the valuation. Otherwise, telephone the registrar of the company who will be able to give the value of the dividend. The dividend per share may be a gross figure in which case multiply it by the number of shares held by the deceased and deduct tax at 10 per cent to arrive at the net figure which will appear on the dividend cheque.

The value of unit trust units can be obtained from the fund manager of the relevant unit trust company. If the deceased owned shares in any unquoted companies, write to the company secretary of each one asking for a valuation of the shares at the date of death.

A list of all shares and their values should be included on *Supplementary page D7* (see completed example on pages 228-9). Dividends (the net figure) should be listed separately as shown. Any dividends which were uncashed at the time of death should also be included. The total values are then included in Section F of *Form IHT 200* (see completed example, page 213). If the deceased had a personal equity plan (PEP) or an Individual Savings Account (ISA) its provider can give a valuation as at the date of death.

Businesses

If the deceased had an interest in a business it will need to be valued by the business' accountant, backed up by a copy of the latest accounts, as requested in *Supplementary page D14* of *Form IHT 200*.

Car

A local garage can provide an accurate valuation of the deceased's car. On the other hand, the executors may prefer simply to sell the car soon after the death and use the sale price as the value at the date of death.

Jewellery

An overall valuation will usually be acceptable for jewellery, although if an individual piece is worth more than £500 it should be valued separately. A jeweller can give a valuation, for which he or she will usually charge a fee. You should tell the jeweller that the valuation is needed for probate or Confirmation purposes to ensure you receive an estimate of the price for which he or she could sell the item, not the replacement value, which may be much higher.

Works of art

One way of finding out whether a particular painting or sculpture is of value is to see if it is separately listed on the deceased's home contents insurance policy but that is by no means necessarily full-proof. An art dealer can give a valuation of any works of art. Make it clear you are asking for the price it would fetch at auction at the date of death, not the value for which it should be insured.

Other possessions

There is no need to compile a detailed list of all of the deceased's possessions, including furniture and personal effects. A reasonable and fair estimate of their total value can be given, based on what they might fetch if sold second-hand or, if appropriate, at auction at the date of death, although details of individual items worth over £500 should be given. The Inland Revenue can challenge asset values if they appear particularly low. In the case of a husband and wife, household possessions are generally treated as being held jointly between them, and so their total value should be divided by two to give the value of the deceased's share. Of course, if the deceased owned something outright, the entire value of the item is considered part of the deceased's estate for inheritance tax purposes.

National Savings

There is a special procedure for National Savings accounts. The executor must complete *Form NSA 904* (available at post offices) and send it to the address given on the form for that type of account. For National Savings certificates, the executor will need to write to National Savings asking for a letter confirming the value of the certificates held by the deceased at the date of death. In England and Wales, the Probate Registry will need to see this letter.

Premium Bonds

You must notify the Premium Bonds Office, by writing to Premium Bonds, National Savings and Investments, Blackpool FY3 9YP, of the holder's death. Bonds can either be encashed or they can remain in the prize draw for 12 months after the death. If any prize is won, it can be claimed in the usual way by returning when appropriate the winning bond to the Bonds and Stock Office, and the prize will belong to the estate to be distributed under the deceased's Will, or the intestacy if there is no Will. As long as the value of the bonds and any prize money does not exceed £5,000, there is normally no need to provide a copy of the grant of probate or Confirmation to receive payment. Premium Bonds are valued at their face value. They should also be listed on the National Savings *Form NSA 904*.

Outstanding salary or pension payments

If the deceased was employed at the time of death, a letter must be sent to his or her employer notifying them of the death and asking whether any salary or other payments are outstanding. However, the employer may need to see a copy of the grant of probate or Confirmation before paying such payments to the executors.

If the deceased belonged to a union or trade association, there may be a death benefit payable to his or her family. Likewise, if the deceased was receiving a pension, the scheme administrator or pension provider must be notified of the death and outstanding pension payments claimed.

Outstanding salary or pension payments should be included in *Form IHT 200* as an asset of the estate. If the deceased was a member of an occupational pension scheme, a lump sum death benefit may be payable and you should write to the scheme administrator or pension provider to find out if that is the case.

Some benefits payable by an employer or a pension fund may be discretionary and not form part of the deceased's estate on death. This means that they do not pass under the deceased's Will or the intestacy and will not be subject to IHT. These benefits would not need to be included in the *Form IHT 200*.

Life insurance and pension policies

Write to the life insurance company or pension provider to notify them of the date of death, stating the policy number and enclosing a copy of a registrar's copy of the death certificate. Ask what sum is payable on the death and whether it was written in trust for any named person. If it was, the proceeds may be paid direct to that person on production of the death certificate. If not, the proceeds, including any bonuses, will generally be included as part of the deceased's estate and must be included in *Form IHT 200*. Sometimes, the policy will be linked to a loan or mortgage, in which case the proceeds will be paid directly to the creditor, any excess being paid to the estate.

Taxes and bills

If the deceased paid income tax under PAYE (Pay As You Earn system) and/or received interest net of tax on bank or building society accounts, there may be a tax refund to claim. On the other hand, if income has been paid gross, or the deceased was a higher rate taxpayer, there may be additional income tax to pay. If the deceased sold any shares, for example, there may also be capital gains tax to pay. In any event, the deceased's tax inspector must be informed of the death. He or she will send a tax return to be completed by the executors, relating to the period up to the time of death. Any tax refund is an asset of the estate (and any additional tax due is a liability of the estate) and must be included in *Form IHT 200*.

A refund of Council Tax may be due. The deceased's home will be exempt from Council Tax if it is left empty from the date of death until probate or Confirmation has been granted, and for a further six months from the date of the grant. If the death leaves just one other person living in the property, the 25 per cent discount for single occupation may be claimed from the date of death. Any refund of Council Tax in respect of a period before the date of death must be included in *Form IHT 200* as an asset of the estate.

Social Security payments

If the deceased was receiving a state retirement pension, the local DSS office should be notified of the death. The pension book should be sent with your letter inquiring whether there are any pension payments uncollected by the deceased. Any underpaid pension will be a debt due to the deceased and must be included in *Form IHT 200* as an asset of the estate. If the deceased was receiving any other state benefits, these will also need to be stopped and any outstanding payments due up to the date of death claimed.

Foreign property

The value in sterling of property owned by the deceased outside the UK or debts owed to him or her by any resident outside the UK must be reported to the Probate Registry or Capital Taxes Office in *Supplementary page D15* of *Form IHT 200*.

Chapter 24:
Applying for a grant

The forms - England and Wales

The forms necessary to apply for a grant of probate are available free of charge from the Personal Applications Department of the Principal Probate Registry in London or from the District Probate Registries (see chapter 26 for details) and from the Inland Revenue's Capital Taxes Office (CTO, tel: 0845 234 1020).

Depending on the estate of the deceased, the forms to be completed are as below. Completed examples are provided in this book for guidance when filling in your own. These are based on two fictional estates that exemplify which forms are completed depending on the estate: Edward John Scott's and Michael Stephen Brown's.

1. *Form PA1* asks for basic information about the deceased and for the names and addresses of the executors.

2. *Form IHT 200* or *Form IHT 205* enable the Probate Registry to determine the probate fee and the CTO any inheritance tax and interest.

3. *Supplementary pages* to be completed with *IHT 200* to give the Inland Revenue further details of the deceased's assets.

The Probate Registries issue *Forms PA1* and *IHT 205*, whilst the CTO issues *Form IHT 200* and its supplementary pages. (You will also receive *Forms* **PA2**, **IHT 213** and **IHT 206**; these contain guidance on completing *PA1*, *IHT 200* and *IHT 205*, respectively.)

Note: Probate forms must be sent by post to a Controlling Probate Registry (see chapter 26); they should not be sent to a local office, even if you want to be interviewed at a local office.

Before looking at the forms in detail, familiarise yourself with the steps and forms involved in obtaining a grant of probate by going through the flowcharts on pages 118-9.

Before probate appointment

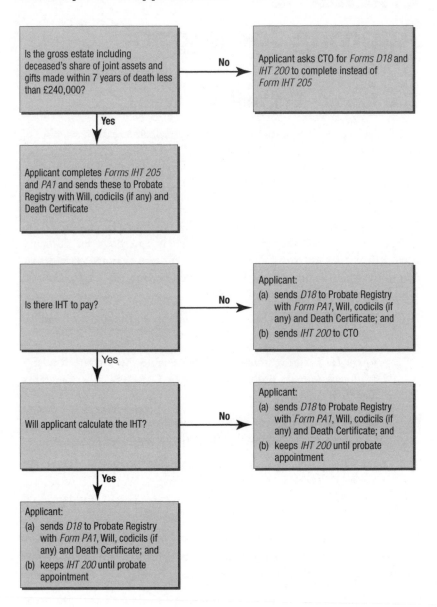

Is the gross estate including deceased's share of joint assets and gifts made within 7 years of death less than £240,000?

No → Applicant asks CTO for *Forms D18* and *IHT 200* to complete instead of *Form IHT 205*

Yes ↓

Applicant completes *Forms IHT 205* and *PA1* and sends these to Probate Registry with Will, codicils (if any) and Death Certificate

---

Is there IHT to pay?

No → Applicant:
(a) sends *D18* to Probate Registry with *Form PA1*, Will, codicils (if any) and Death Certificate; and
(b) sends *IHT 200* to CTO

Yes ↓

Will applicant calculate the IHT?

No → Applicant:
(a) sends *D18* to Probate Registry with *Form PA1*, Will, codicils (if any) and Death Certificate; and
(b) keeps *IHT 200* until probate appointment

Yes ↓

Applicant:
(a) sends *D18* to Probate Registry with *Form PA1*, Will, codicils (if any) and Death Certificate; and
(b) keeps *IHT 200* until probate appointment

After probate appointment

The probate fee is paid at the probate appointment. If the applicant has completed a *Form IHT 205*, the Probate Registry will issue the grant by post after the appointment and without any further formalities. However, where the application requires a *Form IHT 200*, there are further formalities as set out below before the Probate Registry can issue the grant.

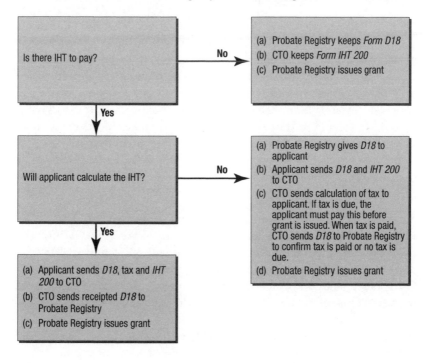

Form PA1 – Probate Application Form (see page 196 for completed example, Edward John Scott's estate).

Section 1 asks which Probate Registry or local office you wish to be interviewed at.

Section 2 asks for the deceased's full name, address, occupation, dates of birth and death, age and marital status and details of any assets of the estate which are held in a name other than the deceased's.

Section 3 asks whether there is a Will and whether a gift is made under it to a person under 18. If so, the executors (or the trustees if the Will appoints trustees) will hold the minor beneficiary's gift until the beneficiary is 18. Question 4 asks for the names of any executors and, if any of the named executors are not applying for probate, why that is the case. If a named executor gives reason D ('does not wish to apply now but may later'), the Probate Registry will provide a power reserved letter for him or her to sign. Where only one executor is taking out the grant it may be prudent for a non-acting executor to sign a power reserved letter, even if it is not anticipated that he or she will want to apply at any stage, in case the acting executor dies or becomes incapacitated before the administration of the estate is complete.

Section 4 asks for details of the deceased's relatives. This will be relevant if there is no Will, as the list of relatives follows the order of entitlement to take out a grant of letters of administration on an intestacy. The list also helps in determining who should inherit where there is an intestacy or a partial intestacy (i.e. where the Will fails to dispose of all the deceased's estate). Note that the list does not include the surviving spouse, who would be the first person entitled to take out the grant on an intestacy; those details are included at question 9 in Section 5. Questions 4, 5 and 6 of Section 4 only need to be answered if the deceased left a Will dated before 4th April 1988 (or died before that date). The relevance of this is explained on page 98.

Section 5 asks for details of those applying to take out the grant. The executor whose name and address are given at questions 1-4 will be the first applicant to whom all correspondence will be addressed. There is space underneath for the name and address of the other executors. Questions 7 and 8 ask about the first applicant's relationship to the deceased. This information is needed for the oath which will be sworn at the Probate Registry on application for the grant. More importantly, in the case of an intestacy, this information verifies that the applicant is the person entitled to take out the grant of letters of administration.

Form IHT 205 Short Form for Personal Applicants (see page 200 for completed example, Michael Stephen Brown's estate).

If you can answer 'no' to all the Preliminary Questions on page 2 of this form there is no need to complete *Form IHT 200*; continue to answer the questions on pages 3 and 4. If any of the answers to the preliminary questions is 'yes', *IHT 200* must be completed, in which case you should answer only the questions on page 2 of *Form IHT 205* and send it to the Probate Registry with *Form IHT 200*. *Form IHT 206* contains notes to help you with *Form IHT 205*.

The forms - Scotland

The forms necessary to apply for a grant of Confirmation are available free of charge from the Sheriff Clerk's Office of the Sheriff Court in the area where the deceased was domiciled at the date of death.

If the estate is a 'small estate', or is an 'excepted estate', then to obtain Confirmation, only *Form C1* (with *continuation Form C2*, if necessary) is required to be completed. For an estate that is neither a small estate nor an excepted estate, it is necessary *in addition to Form C1*, for *Form IHT 200* to be completed.

Excepted estate

The estate will be an excepted estate if *all* the following conditions apply:

1. The deceased was domiciled in the United Kingdom at death.

2. The total gross value of the estate before deduction of any debts, together with the value of any gifts described at point 5 below, does not exceed £240,000.

3. The estate consists only of property which passes under the deceased's Will or intestacy, or by nomination, or joint assets passing beneficially by survivorship. (Where any of the value of an estate relates to joint assets passing by survivorship, it is the value of the deceased's beneficial interest in that property that counts towards the £240,000 limit.)

4. Any assets situated outside the United Kingdom have a total value of not more than £100,000.

5. The total gross value of any lifetime transfers made within seven years of the deceased's death that

    •   consist only of cash or quoted shares or securities and

    •   are not covered by any appropriate exemptions

    is not more than £100,000.

The estate is *not* an excepted estate where the deceased:

•   had within seven years of death made a lifetime transfer other than of cash or quoted shares or securities;

•   had within seven years of the death made a lifetime transfer that was chargeable at the time it was made, for example, to a company or to a discretionary trust, made a gift with reservation of benefit which either continued until death or ceased within seven years before the death. A gift with reservation is one where the person receiving the gift does not fully own it, or where the person making the gift either reserves or takes some benefit from it. A simple example is where a person gave a house to his or her child then continued to live in the house;

- had the right to receive the benefit from assets held under a trust either at, or within seven years before, the death. A person has the right to receive a benefit from assets held under a trust when he or she:

    - receives the income from assets (for example, interest from a building society account or dividends from stocks and shares);

    - receives a fixed payment each year, often in instalments; or

    - has the right to use the trust assets (for example, live in a house and use the contents without paying rent).

If you are not sure whether any transfers made by the deceased fall within these exceptions, you should contact the Inland Revenue Helpline. If you think the estate is an excepted estate, you should tick the appropriate box at the foot of the last page of *Form C1*.

Small estates

A small estate is an estate where the gross value of the estate, including any gifts, does not exceed £25,000. You should tick the appropriate box on the last page of *Form C1* if the estate is a small estate.

Completed examples of *Forms C1* (and *continuation Form C2*) and *Form IHT 200* (and related *'D' forms* which are effectively supplementary pages to *IHT 200*) are provided in this book for guidance when filling in your own forms.

C1 Account — this provides particulars of the deceased and whether the deceased died testate or intestate.

IHT 200 — enables you (and the Capital Taxes Office) to determine whether any inheritance tax is payable.

If inheritance tax is payable on an estate then payment should be submitted to the Capital Taxes Office at Meldrum House, 15 Drumsheugh Gardens, Edinburgh, EH3 7UG along with both *Form IHT*

200 and the *C1 Account*. The *C1 Account* will be receipted by the Capital Taxes Office and returned to you.

If there is no inheritance tax payable then *Form IHT 200* should be submitted to the Capital Taxes Office at Meldrum House, 15 Drumsheugh Gardens, Edinburgh, EH3 7UG *without* the *C1 Account*.

Bond of Caution - In the case of an application for Confirmation by an executor-dative, before applying for Confirmation it is normally necessary for a *Bond of Caution* to be obtained from an insurance company. This *Bond of Caution* is effectively a guarantee given by the insurance company to the Court that the executor-dative will distribute the deceased's estate properly in terms of the Law of intestate succession. For such a *Bond of Caution* a single premium is payable which is likely to be in the region of £300 or more depending on the values and circumstances. In granting such a *Bond of Caution*, the insurance company may require certain conditions to be complied with (such as the need to obtain clearance from the DSS that there has been no overpayment of benefits or that a minor beneficiary's share of the estate should be held until the beneficiary attains the age of 18 years).

Where the executor-dative is the spouse of the deceased, and as such is entitled to the whole of the intestate estate of the deceased, then there is no requirement for a *Bond of Caution*.

Application - Scotland

Application for Confirmation is made to The Sheriff Clerk of the Sheriff Court in the area in which the deceased had been domiciled at his or her death by:

1. *C1 Account* (receipted where IHT is payable).

2. Will (docquetted with reference to the *C1 Account*) or *Bond of Caution*, as appropriate.

3. The appropriate fee: for a gross estate under £5,000: nil.
   For a gross estate not exceeding £50,000: £81.
   For a gross estate exceeding £50,000: £114.
   A charge of £3 is payable for each Certificate of Confirmation requested.

4. Request for Confirmation and any required Certificates of Confirmation.

The forms - England, Wales & Scotland

Form IHT 200 Full Account for Personal Applicants applies to estates both in England and Wales and in Scotland (see page 213 for completed example, Edward John Scott's estate).

The questions on this form are similar to those on the English *Form IHT 205* and the Scottish *C1 Account* but they require fuller details. There may be a number of supplementary pages to complete with the *Form IHT 200* as in our example. If there is insufficient space for all the information asked for, you should attach a separate sheet of paper and include the total on *Form IHT 200* itself. *Form IHT 213* will help you answer the questions. If the estate includes land or buildings *Supplementary page D12* should also be completed. If it includes stocks and shares, list the details on *Supplementary page D7*. *Supplementary pages D4, D3, D5* and *D6* deal with nominated property, gifts, assets held in trust and death benefits payable under pension policies. These may not appear to be part of the estate, but they may need to be taken into account in order to calculate inheritance tax. *Supplementary page D4* also deals with jointly-held property and land and buildings (whether inside the UK or not).

The inheritance tax on some types of property may be paid by instalments (see page 127) and page 5 of the form includes a box to be ticked, should you wish to do that.

In sections H and J on pages 6 and 7 of *IHT 200* the executors have the choice of either calculating any inheritance tax themselves or leaving it to the CTO to work out (by leaving these sections blank).

All the executors should read the Declaration on page 8 of *Form IHT 200* and sign it. (**NB** This differs from the *C1 Accounts* that in Scotland require to be signed by one executor only.)

Supplementary page D7 Stocks and Shares (see page 228 for completed example, Edward John Scott's estate).

If the deceased owned stocks or shares, the details of those holdings should be entered on this form; only the total is carried to *Form IHT 200*.

The notes at the top of the form tell you the order in which you should list the holdings. See chapter 23 for the method of valuing the holdings.

Column 1 asks for the name of the company and types of shares, e.g. the type of share, stock or unit trust, and its nominal value, e.g. 'ordinary 25p shares', '12½ per cent unsecured loan stock' or 'managed fund units'.

Column 2 asks for the number of shares or amount of stock held.

The market price per share/unit should be included in Column 3. The figure in Column 4 is the value of the total holding, calculated by multiplying the number of shares/units in Column 2 by the price in Column 3.

Any dividends or interest due at death should be included in Column 5.

*Supplementary page D12 **Land, Buildings and Interests in Land*** (see page 233 for completed example, Edward John Scott's estate).

Complete this form if the deceased owned any land; only the total amount will be carried to *Form IHT 200*.

You should use separate supplementary pages if there was any land owned in England and Wales, Scotland or Northern Ireland. Either ask the Probate Registry or Sheriff Clerk for another form or photocopy the original.

The notes at the top tell you what to put in each column. If the property is let, attach copies of the tenancy agreements described in Column D.

Column F asks for the 'Open Market Value'; do not deduct the amount of any mortgage which has been or will need to be repaid. If the deceased owned, for example, the house in his or her sole name, record the gross value of the entire property, even if the spouse or someone else is claiming an interest in part of it. If the deceased was a joint owner of the property, you need only include the value of the deceased's share in Column F (in the example of Michael Stephen Brown's estate on page 234, both he and his wife, Frances Brown, owned the house as beneficial joint tenants - the deceased's half-share in the house passes to his wife by survivorship).

At the Probate Registry - England & Wales

About three weeks after sending the probate forms, as set out in the flowcharts, the executors will be contacted with a time and date for an interview. All executors need to attend in order to swear an oath, which is needed to apply for the grant of probate. They will also need to produce the testator's original Will. Where the executors have completed a *Form IHT 205*, this is signed at the Probate Registry interview.

Probate fees must be paid at this interview. It may therefore be necessary for executors to arrange for a loan or overdraft to pay these fees and the IHT due on the issue of the grant. Probate fees may be paid by cheque, banker's draft, postal order or in cash. On personal applications, the probate fee is currently £130, unless the net estate is less than £5,000, in which case no probate fee is payable for the grant.

At the interview, the executors will be asked to swear that the information on the oath and the Inland Revenue account is correct. It is a good idea to take back-up files to verify facts and figures. If all the information is exactly as the executors have previously submitted, they are asked to sign the account, swear to the facts set out in the oath, which refers to the Will and put their signatures on the Will. Then the commissioner handling the case adds his or her signature to the oath and Will. The executors may then order as many copies of the grant of probate, each bearing the court's seal, as are necessary to notify all the parties first informed of the death with copies of the death certificate. Copies currently cost £1 each. If there are further questions before the grant can be issued, the executors could be asked to return to the Registry for another interview.

In the case of an intestacy, the grant issued is a 'grant of letters of administration'. The administrator should order as many copies of the grant as are necessary, as above.

If there is no inheritance tax due, the grant will be issued almost immediately. Assuming there are no further questions, the grant of probate with a copy of the Will attached and the copies of the grant will arrive by post. The grant is proof to the public that the executors can realise the deceased's assets, collect from the deceased's debtors and distribute the assets as determined by the Will. Both the Will and the grant of probate are public documents.

The executors can now send a grant of probate to all parties that first received the death certificate, requesting whatever money is due to be sent to the executors. This money is deposited into the executors' bank account, from which debts of the deceased are paid.

At the Sheriff Court - Scotland

Within about two weeks after submitting your application for Confirmation to the Sheriff Clerk in the Sheriff Court concerned, the Sheriff Clerk will send to you the Confirmation (together with any certificates of Confirmation ordered).

The grant of Confirmation is proof to the public that the executors can realise the deceased's estate, collect from the deceased's debtors and distribute the assets, as determined by the Will. Both the Will and the grant of Confirmation are public documents. The executors can now send the Confirmation, or a certificate of Confirmation, to all parties concerned, requesting whatever money is due to the estate. This money can be deposited into the executors' bank account from which debts of the deceased can be paid.

Inheritance tax

The executors can calculate the tax themselves by working through the worksheet *IHT/WS*, and completing forms *IHT 200* and *D18* accordingly. If the executors are not sure how to complete *Form IHT 200*, the Inheritance Tax Helpline (tel: 0845 30 20 900) can be contacted for assistance in completing the form.

If the executors do not wish to calculate the tax, the CTO will do this for them (see flowcharts for details).

The Inland Revenue exempts all property left to the surviving spouse or to charity and the first £255,000 (from 6th April 2003) of the estate not left to the spouse or charity (assuming there have been no gifts made by the deceased in the seven-year period prior to death; if there have been any gifts in the seven-year period before death, you should declare these in *Form D3*). The excess bears tax at 40 per cent. You will see in the example *Form D3* on page 224 that the lifetime gifts made by Mr Scott are exempt from inheritance tax. If the total value of all gifts in any one tax year does not exceed £3,000, then they will all be free of inheritance tax. If the total value of gifts in any tax year is less than £3,000, then the surplus of this relief can be carried forward to the next tax year only and be used against gifts made in that later tax year, once the £3,000 available for the later tax year has been used up. This relief is known as the annual exemption.

The inheritance tax owed on buildings or land, a business or a share in a business, shares giving a controlling interest in a quoted company and some unquoted shares can, with prior approval, be paid in 10 equal annual instalments (although interest is payable on these instalments if the asset is land or buildings). Inheritance tax on other assets must be paid before the grant of probate or Confirmation can be issued and interest is charged on any inheritance tax outstanding from the end of the sixth month after the death (except where it is being paid by non-interest bearing instalments).

Changes to the amount of inheritance tax

Even after probate or Confirmation has been granted, the Inland Revenue may ask further questions about the assets and liabilities of the estate, and values may have to be negotiated. For example, the Inland Revenue may challenge the value reported on *Form IHT 200* for a house or for unquoted shares. This could result in more inheritance tax being payable.

If the executors discover an asset or debt of the deceased which they did not know about before they applied for probate or Confirmation, they must report it to the Inland Revenue as soon as possible after its discovery. This may also change the amount of inheritance tax payable.

Once the inheritance tax position has been settled, the executors should ask the Inland Revenue for *Form 30*, an application to be discharged from further inheritance tax. Two copies completed and signed by *all* the executors are needed by the Inland Revenue. One copy is returned certifying that no further inheritance tax is payable. The executors can then distribute the estate. However, if any further assets come to light subsequently, these too will need to be reported to the Inland Revenue, as the discharge from inheritance tax would not cover them.

Raising money to pay inheritance tax and the probate fee or Confirmation dues

Because an executor cannot draw on the funds in the deceased's bank account until he or she can show entitlement by producing the grant, the executor may need to borrow the necessary funds to pay inheritance tax and the probate fee or Confirmation dues. There are, however, some assets which an institution may be willing to release before the grant of probate or Confirmation is available, in order to pay the inheritance tax, and some assets that may be realised without producing the grant of probate or Confirmation. The tax may be covered, or partly covered, from such sources as an alternative to borrowing. The following are assets which the executors may be able to use in this way.

1. **National Savings.** In England and Wales, if the deceased had a National Savings account, National Savings certificates or Premium Bonds, National Savings may issue a cheque in favour of the Inland Revenue to cover the inheritance tax payable on the estate or part of it. The executors should explain to the Probate Registry at their interview that they would like to use funds of the deceased's National Savings account to pay the tax. The Registry will issue a note stating that the executors have made a personal application and showing the amount of probate fees and inheritance tax payable.

The Registry then sends this note to the relevant National Savings office, which will send the cheque for the tax and the probate fee to the Probate Registry directly. Any remaining balance on the deceased's National Savings account will be paid to the executors and any remaining National Savings certificates and Premium Bonds can be encashed once the grant has been obtained.

2. **Funds payable to others without grant of probate or Confirmation** (see *Is a grant of probate or Confirmation necessary?* in chapter 22). Consider utilising funds from nominated property, joint property or lump-sum death benefits from pension funds, life assurance companies and friendly societies which have been written in trust for another person. However, such funds or assets would belong to the person to whom they are payable, rather than to the estate, and the executors would need to borrow from that person if they wished to use those funds to pay the inheritance tax.

3. **Pension funds and friendly societies.** Funds of up to £5,000 from some pension funds and friendly societies.

4. **Building society or Girobank.** Building societies and the Girobank are often willing to release money to pay inheritance tax and the probate fee or Confirmation dues, but they may want to send the money direct to the Inland Revenue at the Capital Taxes Office or HM Paymaster General to ensure that it is used for this purpose. The Girobank may be willing to lend the executors a sum up to the balance on the deceased's account to pay inheritance tax and the probate fee or Confirmation dues. The funds required for the tax may also be sent direct to the Capital Taxes Office using form D20 (see page 105).

5. **Other assets.** Furniture and other personal possessions of the deceased may be sold by executors, who are entitled to sell the assets of the estate from the date of death, but in England and Wales, not administrators, who are only entitled to do so once they have the grant of letters of administration.

6. **Stocks and shares.** If held through a stockbroker's nominee company.

If insufficient assets are realisable before the grant is issued, the executors will have to borrow the money to pay the inheritance tax. Some sources might include (see over):

1. **Loan from the deceased's bank.** A bank will normally make a loan to the executors, although a fee will be payable based on the size of the loan and, of course, interest will be charged. The executors may claim income tax relief on the interest payment for the first year of the administration in respect of a loan for the inheritance tax payable on personal property.

2. **Loan from a beneficiary.** A beneficiary may be able and willing to lend the money to the estate to pay the inheritance tax, particularly if the bank interest and fee would be paid out of cash that he or she would otherwise receive.

Chapter 25: Administering an estate

Distribution of gifts and legacies

To satisfy any debts of the estate, it is the assets forming part of the residuary estate that are used first. If there are still outstanding debts when the residuary estate has been used up, cash legacies are reduced proportionately to meet the debt. If there are unpaid debts outstanding, specific items left as legacies under the Will need to be sold. Once all the debts are paid and the assets are all accounted for and collected the executors are in a position to distribute the estate in accordance with the Will.

As each personal effect, gift and legacy of money is distributed to the beneficiaries of the estate, the executors should ask each beneficiary to sign a receipt. The receipt should record the amount of money or description of the gift, the names of the executors, the name and signature of the beneficiary and the date. The beneficiary should be invited to keep a copy of the receipt. The Will may contain a clause saying that, if there is a gift to a child, his or her parent or guardian can sign the receipt. Otherwise, gifts to minors should be invested by the executor in an account until the child reaches 18 (the age of 'majority').

Transfer of assets

If assets are to be transferred to a beneficiary (rather than being sold and the proceeds paid to him or her), the method of transfer will differ according to the asset. Household and personal effects may be physically handed over, without any legal paperwork.

Shares will need to be transferred using a *Stock Transfer Form* (see completed example on page 235). This should be completed and signed by all executors and sent to the registrar of the company, together with the share certificate and an office copy of the grant of probate, or Certificate of Confirmation, as appropriate. Alternatively, a stockbroker or bank would be able to prepare the stock transfer forms and send them to the registrars. If a shareholding is to be split between two or more beneficiaries, a separate form of stock transfer is needed for each beneficiary. No stamp duty is payable on the transfer of shares from executors to a beneficiary, provided that the appropriate certificate on the back of the form has been completed and signed by the executors. Where the shares are given in the Will as a specific legacy, the appropriate category to be inserted in the certificate is 'B', and if they are part of the residue, the appropriate category is 'E'. If the shares are registered in the name of a stockbroker's or bank's nominee company, the executors need not complete stock transfer forms but should write to the nominee company, giving it the name and address of the beneficiary of the shares and instructing it to hold the shares on behalf of the beneficiary in future.

If a house or flat is to be transferred to a beneficiary, the procedure in England and Wales differs according to whether the title is registered or unregistered. In England and Wales, the document needed to transfer the ownership of the property is called an assent.

In the case of registered land title(s) in England and Wales, you need to use Land Registry *Form AS1 Assent of whole of registered title(s)*, available from legal stationers. If only part of the registered land title is being transferred, you will need to complete a *Form AS3*. The completed form needs to be signed by each executor in the presence of a witness and by the beneficiary to whom the property is being transferred (see example on page 206). The executors should then send it, together with an office copy of the grant of probate, the land certificate and the Land Registry fee to the Land Registry so they can register the new owner. The Land Registry fee will vary according to the value of the property, net of any outstanding mortgage (if it has not been repaid following the death). The current scale of fees for registering an assent is as follows:

Value net of mortgage	Fee
£0–£100,000	£40
£100,001–£200,000	£50
£200,001–£500,000	£70
£500,001–£1,000,000	£100
£1,000,001 and over	£200

If the land is in England and Wales and unregistered the title deeds will consist of a number of deeds and documents including the deed (*a conveyance*) whereby the property was transferred to the deceased. In the case of unregistered land it is best to seek the advice of a solicitor as the title to the property would then have to be registered at the Land Registry as a first registration application.

In Scotland, whether the title of heritable property (i.e. land or buildings) in Scotland is registered in the Land Registry (of Scotland) or not, a docket on the Confirmation or Certificate of Confirmation can be a method of transferring title to a beneficiary (either under a Will or in terms of legal rights or in accordance with the Law of Intestate Succession in Scotland). See the form of Docket on page 212. The *Confirmation* or *Certificate of Confirmation* with completed docket should be held with the titles of the property. It may be prudent for preservation purposes to have such docketed Confirmation (or Certificate of Confirmation) registered in the Books of Council and Session on application to the Keeper of the Registers of Scotland at Meadowbank House, 153 London Road, Edinburgh EH8 7AU. A docket is not needed if the title deed contains a survivorship destination as the title will automatically have transferred to the survivor on the death of the first to die.

Final accounts

The careful records that have been kept since the date of death should now be organised in a neat and easily-read format for approval by each beneficiary.

A word of caution: In England and Wales, for a period of six months following the grant of probate, claims may be made under the Inheritance (Provision for Family and Dependants) Act 1975, for example, by a member of the deceased's family who feels he or she has not been properly provided for in the Will. In England and Wales, it is therefore wise not to distribute the residue of the estate until six months has passed. If such a claim is made the executors should seek the advice of a solicitor.

In Scotland, it may be prudent to delay distribution of the estate until the expiry of six months after the death to allow for any claims to be made against the estate. If the executor were to distribute prior to the expiry of that six-month period, he or she may be personally liable for any claims intimated in that period.

After the residuary beneficiaries (or those entitled under the intestacy laws) have signed off on the accounts, the estate is completed. The executors' bank account can be closed and whatever money remains is given to those entitled under the Will or intestacy laws.

Paperwork should be kept on file for 12 years after final distribution. In the event that the deceased left someone a life interest or liferent in the estate, the paperwork should be kept for 12 years after the final distribution to whoever inherits after the death of the last person with a life interest or liferent.

Taxation of the estate

Income from the estate will be liable to income tax from the date of death to the date it has been fully administered. The estate will be assessed to income tax on all income received gross at the basic rate, but with no personal allowance. No further income tax will be payable if all income (for example, bank interest, dividends, etc.) has been paid net of tax. Gains (relative to date of death values) on any sales of shares after death may be liable to capital gains tax. The executors' annual exemption for capital gains tax is the same, for the tax year in which the death occurred and the following two years, as any individual's annual exemption (£7,900 for the tax year 2003/04). However, gains in an estate are taxed at 34 per cent. Thus the executors should liaise with the beneficiaries before selling assets which are likely to make a taxable gain to see whether the capital gains tax can be reduced by using the beneficiaries' rates of tax and exemptions. If in doubt, the executors should seek professional advice. When the executors notify the Tax Inspector for the deceased's tax district of the death, the Inspector will send *Form 920* which asks for information as to who will be entitled to the residue of the estate, whether there will be any trust continuing after the estate has been wound up and whether the executor expects to receive any untaxed income or make any capital gains. On the basis of that form, the Inspector will issue the correct tax returns to be filled in for the estate.

The executors may also need to issue a certificate of tax deduction (*Form R185 (Estate Income)*, also available from the tax office) to the beneficiary who is entitled to the residue of the estate. This form shows the gross income received by the estate during the tax year, the tax paid by the executors on that income and the resulting net figure. As long as the residue is not held in trust, the income of the estate is treated as the income of the beneficiary, who will report the income on his or her tax return, and *Form R185 (Estate Income)* is evidence that tax has already been paid on it. If the beneficiary is a non-taxpayer, he or she can reclaim the tax. If he or she is a higher rate taxpayer, he or she will be assessable to additional tax.

Succession on intestacy

For England and Wales, refer to the flowchart opposite and the text on pages 4-7.

For Scotland, see pages 7-8.

Succession on intestacy in England and Wales

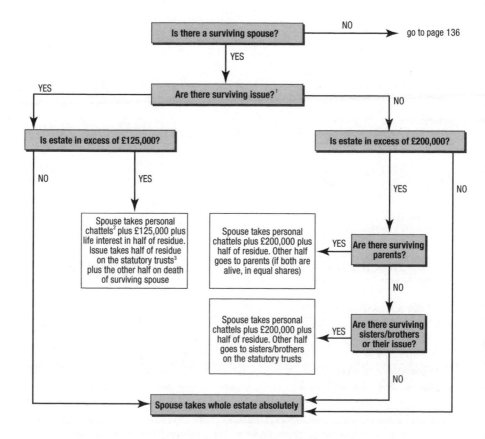

1 **'ISSUE'** Children, grandchildren or remoter lineal descendants of the intestate.

2 **'PERSONAL CHATTELS'** Under s.55 (1) (x) of the Administration of Estates Act 1925, 'personal chattels' includes: horses, motor cars, garden implements, domestic animals, furniture, linen, china, glass, books, pictures, musical and scientific instruments, jewellery, household and personal articles, food and drink, but does not include any chattels used at the date of death for business purposes nor money or securities.

3 **'THE STATUTORY TRUSTS'** Those children of the intestate who are alive at his or her death inherit in equal shares although if a child is under 18 he or she must reach

the age of 18 or marry under that age in order to inherit. If any child dies before the intestate, leaving children of his or her own, those children (i.e. the intestate's grandchildren) will take *per stirpes* i.e. they will take their parents' share equally between them (provided they reach the age of 18 or marry under that age). If remoter issue predeceased the intestate leaving their own issue, this process would continue down the generations. References to the children of the intestate should be read as references to brothers, sisters, aunts or uncles as appropriate, where any of those classes are stated to inherit on the statutory trusts. See illustration of *per stirpes* distribution on page 136.

Succession on intestacy in England and Wales continued

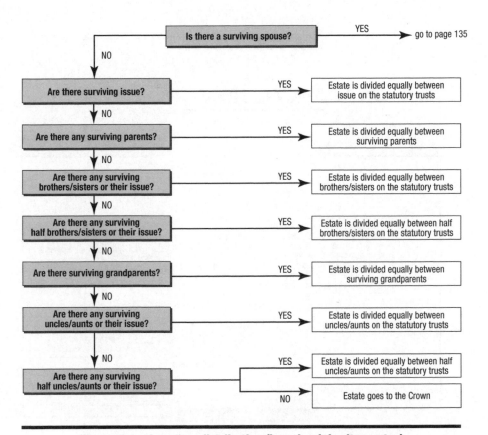

Illustration of *per stirpes* distribution (ignoring inheritance tax)

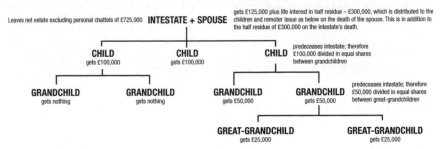

Chapter 26: Probate appendices

For use in England and Wales

Probate Registries and local offices

Controlling Probate offices are open 9.30am–4.00pm. Opening times for local offices may be different. You can get addresses and hours for local offices by calling the Probate Registries.

Controlling Probate Registry	*Local offices*
Bangor Council Offices Ffordd Gwynedd Bangor LL57 1DT Tel. 01248 362410	Rhyl Wrexham
Birmingham The Priory Courts 33 Bull Street Birmingham B4 6DU Tel. 0121 681 3400/3414	Coventry Birmingham Kidderminster Northampton Wolverhampton
Bodmin Market Street Bodmin PL31 2JW Tel. 01208 72279	Truro Plymouth
Brighton William Street Brighton BN2 2LG Tel. 01273 684071	Chichester Horsham Hastings
Bristol The Crescent Centre Temple Back Bristol BS1 6EP Tel. 0117 927 3915/926 4619	Bath Weston-Super-Mare

Controlling Probate Registry	*Local offices*
Cardiff	Bridgend
Probate Registry of Wales	Newport
PO Box 474	Pontypridd
2 Park Street	
Cardiff CF10 1TB	
Tel. 029 2037 6479	
Carlisle	
Courts of Justice	
Earl Street	
Carlisle CA1 1DJ	
Tel. 01228 521751	
Carmarthen	Aberystwyth
14 King Street	Haverfordwest
Carmarthen	Swansea
Dyfed SA31 1BL	
Tel. 01267 236238	
Chester	
5th Floor, Hamilton House	
Hamilton Place	
Chester CH1 2DA	
Tel. 01244 345082	
Exeter	Barnstaple
Finance House	Newton Abbot
Barnfield Road	Taunton
Exeter EX1 1QR	Yeovil
Tel. 01392 274515	
Gloucester	Cheltenham
2nd Floor	Hereford
Combined Court Building	Worcester
Kimbrose Way	
Gloucester GL1 2DG	
Tel. 01452 522585	
Ipswich	Chelmsford
Ground Floor	Colchester
8 Arcade Street	
Ipswich IP4 1DN	
Tel. 01473 253724/259261	

Controlling Probate Registry

Lancaster
Mitre House
Church Street.
Lancaster LA1 1HE
Tel. 01524 36625

Leeds
3rd Floor, Coronet House
Queen Street
Leeds LS1 2BA
Tel. 0113 243 1505

Leicester
90 Wellington Street
Leicester LE1 6HG
Tel. 0116 285 3380

Lincoln
360 High Street
Lincoln LN5 7PS
Tel. 01522 523648

Liverpool
The Queen Elizabeth II
Law Courts
Derby Square
Liverpool L2 1XA
Tel. 0151 236 8264

London
Principal Registry
Family Division
First Avenue House
42–49 High Holborn
London WC1V 6NP
Tel. 020 7947 6939
Personal enquiries Room 83

Maidstone
The Law Courts
Barker Road
Maidstone ME16 8EW
Tel. 01622 202048

Local offices

Barrow-in-Furness
Blackpool
Preston
St Helens

Bedford

Southport

Croydon
Edmonton
Harlow
Kingston
Luton
Southend-on-Sea
Woolwich

Canterbury
Tunbridge Wells

Controlling Probate Registry	*Local offices*
Manchester 9th Floor Astley House 23 Quay Street Manchester M3 4AT Tel. 0161 834 4319	Bolton Nelson Oldham Warrington Wigan
Middlesbrough Combined Court Centre Russell Street Middlesbrough TS1 2AE Tel. 01642 340001	
Newcastle-upon-Tyne 2nd Floor Plummer House Croft Street Newcastle-upon-Tyne NE1 6NP Tel. 0191 261 8383	
Norwich Combined Court Building The Law Courts Bishopsgate Norwich NR3 1UR Tel. 01603 728267	Lowestoft Kings Lynn
Nottingham Butt Dyke House 33 Park Row Nottingham NG1 6GR Tel. 0115 941 4288	Derby Mansfield
Oxford The Combined Courts St Aldates Oxford OX1 1LY Tel. 01865 793055	Aylesbury High Wycombe Reading Slough Swindon
Peterborough First Floor, Crown Building Rivergate Peterborough PE1 1EJ Tel. 01733 562802	Cambridge

Controlling Probate Registry   *Local offices*

Sheffield
PO Box 832
The Law Courts
50 West Bar
Sheffield S3 8YR
Tel. 0114 281 2597

Stoke-on-Trent   Crewe
Combined Court Centre   Shrewsbury
Bethesda Street   Stafford
Hanley
Stoke-on-Trent ST1 3BP
Tel. 01782 854065

Winchester   Basingstoke
4th Floor   Bournemouth
Cromwell House   Dorchester
Andover Road   Guildford
Winchester SO23 7EW   Newport I.O.W.
Tel. 01962 863771 (2 lines)   Portsmouth
                                      Salisbury
                                      Southampton

York   Hull
Castle Chambers   Scarborough
Clifford Street
York YO1 2EA
Tel. 01904 666777

For use in Scotland

Sheriff Courts

Aberdeen   **Airdrie**
Castle Street   Graham Street
Aberdeen AB10 1WP   Airdrie ML6 6EE
Tel. 01224 657200   Tel. 01236 751121

Alloa   **Arbroath**
Mar Street   Town House
Alloa FK10 1HR   88 High Street
Tel. 01259 722734   Arbroath D11 1HL
                                      Tel. 01241 876600

Ayr
Wellington Square
Ayr KA7 1EE
Tel. 01292 268474

Banff
Low Street
Banff AB45 1AU
Tel. 01261 812140

Campbeltown
Castle Hill
Campbeltown PA28 6AN
Tel. 01586 552503

Cupar
County Buildings
St Catherine Street
Cupar KY15 4LX
Tel. 01334 652121

Dingwall
Ferry Road
Dingwall
Ross-shire IV15 9QX
Tel. 01349 863153

Dornoch
Castle Street
Dornoch IV25 3FD
Tel. 01862 810224

Dumbarton
Church Street
Dumbarton G82 1QR
Tel. 01389 763266

Dumfries
Buccleuch Street
Dumfries DG1 2AN
Tel. 01387 262334

Dundee
6 West Bell Street
Dundee DD1 9AD
Tel. 01382 229961

Dunfermline
1/6 Carnegie Drive
Dumfermline KY12 7HJ
Tel. 01383 724666

Dunoon
George Street
Dunoon PA23 8BQ
Tel. 01369 704166

Duns
8 Newtown Street
Duns TD11 3DU
Tel. 01361 883719

Edinburgh
Chambers Street
Edinburgh EH1 1LB
Tel. 0131 2252525

Elgin
High Street
Elgin
Moray IV30 1BU
Tel. 01343 542505

Falkirk
Main Street
Camelon
Falkirk FK1 4AR
Tel. 01324 620822

Forfar
Market Street
Forfar DD8 3LA
Tel. 01307 462186

Fort William
High Street
Fort William PH33 6EE
Tel. 01397 702087

Glasgow
PO Box 23
1 Carlton Place
Glasgow G5 9DA
Tel. 0141 4298888

Greenock
1 Nelson Street
Greenock PA15 1TR
Tel. 01475 787073

Haddington
Court Street
Haddinton EH41 3HN
Tel. 0162 0822936

Hamilton
4 Beckford Street
Hamilton ML3 0BT
Tel. 01698 282957

Inverness
The Castle
Inverness IV2 3EG
Tel. 01463 230782

Jedburgh
Castlegate
Jedburgh TD8 6AR
Tel. 01835 863231

Kilmarnock
St Marnock Street
Kilmarnock KA1 1ED
Tel. 01563 543568

Kirkcaldy
Whytescauseway
Kirkcaldy KY1 1XQ
Tel. 01592 260171

Kirkcudbright
High Street
Kirkcudbright DG6 4JW
Tel. 01557 330574

Kirkwall
Watergate
Kirkwall
Orkney KW15 1PD
Tel. 01856 872110

Lanark
Hozier House
Hyndford Road
Lanark
Tel. 01555 661531

Lerwick
King Erik Street
Lerwick
Shetland ZE1 0HD
Tel. 01595 693914

Linlithgow
High Street
Linlithgow EH49 7EQ
Tel. 01506 842922

Lochmaddy
North Uist PA82 5AE
Tel. 01876 500340

Oban
Albany Street
Oban PA34 4AL
Tel. 01631 562414

Paisley
St James Street
Paisley PA3 2AW
Tel. 0141 8875291

Peebles
High Street
Peebles EH45 8SW
Tel. 01721 720204

Perth
Tay Street
Perth PH2 8NL
Tel. 01738 620546

Peterhead
Queen Street
Peterhead AB42 1TP
Tel. 01779 476676

Portree
Somerled Square
Portree
Isle of Skye IV51 9EH
Tel. 01478 612191

Rothesay
Castle Street
Rothesay PA20 9HA
Tel. 01700 502982

Selkirk
Ettrick Terrace
Selkirk TD7 4LE
Tel. 01750 21269

Stirling
Viewfield Place
Stirling FK8 1NH
Tel. 01786 462191

Stonehaven
Dunnottar Avenue
Stonehaven AB3 2JH
Tel. 01569 762758

Stornoway
Lewis Street
Stornoway
Isle of Lewis HS1 2JF
Tel. 01851 702231

Stranraer
Lewis Street
Stranraer DG9 7AA
Tel. 01776 702138

Tain
High Street
Tain IV19 1AB
Tel. 01862 892518

Wick
Bridge Street
Wick KW1 4AJ
Tel. 01955 602846

Example letter to deceased's mortgage lender

Windmill Cottage
Petworth
West Sussex TN20 7XP

27th May 2003

Dear Sirs

Patricia Lacey
2 Allan Gardens
Chichester PO7 2X5
Roll number: A/678123

I am an executor of the estate of Patricia Lacey, who died on 19th May 2003. My two co-executors are Louise Jones of 102 Oakley Road, Guildford, Surrey G9 5TT and Mark Robinson of 52 Mulford Avenue, Winchester SO23 9XT. I enclose a copy of the death certificate, which I would be grateful if you would return to me once you have noted the details.

Please let me know the amount of capital outstanding on the above mortgage and the amount of interest due at the date of death.

Miss Lacey held an endowment policy with County Insurance reference number 3579/246A. Please let me know what sum is payable under the policy following her death and if there will be any surplus remaining after repayment.

Yours faithfully

David Chambers

David Chambers

Example letter to deceased's bank

17 Arundel Way
Bristol BS8 3JQ

30th July 2003

Dear Sirs

Edward John Scott, deceased
Account number: 00034567

I am an executor of the estate of my father, the late Edward John Scott, who died on 27th July 2003. My co-executor is my sister, Rosemary Jane Rayner, who lives at 98 Churchill Road, Swindon SN9 4SZ. I enclose a copy of the death certificate, which I should be grateful if you would return once you have noted the details.

Please would you:

1. Put an immediate stop on all unpaid cheques and standing orders from the above account.

2. Let me know the balance on the account at the date of death and, as a separate figure, any interest accrued but not credited up to that date.

3. Send me a list of any deeds and documents you are holding on Mr Scott's behalf.

4. Let me know the amount of interest paid during the current tax year up to the date of death, whether it was paid gross or net and the amount of any tax deducted.

My sister and I wish to open an executor's account and I should be grateful if you would send me the appropriate forms for us to sign in order to do that.

Yours faithfully

Melanie Scott

Melanie Scott

Glossary

A–C

Absolute ownership — unconditional ownership.

Administrators — in England and Wales, the personal representatives appointed when the deceased dies intestate or where there are no executors able or willing to act.

Adult — under English law, a person over the age of 18 or under Scots law, a person aged 16 or over.

Advance Directives — a written record of decisions about your future health care, given effect by a Living Will.

Assent — document in England and Wales whereby land or buildings are transferred to a beneficiary of an estate.

Attestation clause — the clause at the end of a Will declaring the date and place of signing and the names and designations of the witness or witnesses.

Attorney — a person who has authority to act on behalf of another.

Beneficial joint tenants — in England and Wales, joint holders of property who are treated as a single unit.

Beneficial tenants in common — in England and Wales, joint holders of property with individual shares in the property.

Beneficiary — a person who receives all or part of an estate under a Will or intestacy; a beneficiary may also be the person who receives payment from a life insurance policy or a trust.

Bequeath — to leave a bequest for someone in a Will.

Bequest — a gift of money or property in a Will.

Cancellation by extinction — a bequest is cancelled because you no longer own the gift at the time of your death.

Cancellation by satisfaction — a bequest is cancelled because you have already given the gift to the beneficiary during your lifetime.

Capacity — competence to enter into a legally binding agreement.

C–E

Child — legitimate, illegitimate or adopted child of a parent (excludes step-child).

Codicil — a document that modifies some provision of a Will but does not revoke it.

Confirmation — in Scotland, the court order giving an executor-nominate or executor-dative the right to deal with the deceased's assets.

Continuing Power of Attorney — in Scotland, a power of attorney that remains in effect during the incapacity of the Donor.

Court of Protection — a court that administers the property and affairs of persons of unsound mind.

Delegate — to grant authority to a person to act on behalf of another person.

Devises — in English law, gifts of land made in a Will.

Disclaim — to refuse or renounce a right or authority.

Dispone — to transfer or give.

Docket on Confirmation — the docket used in Scotland to transfer the title of a dwellinghouse or land or buildings to the beneficiary of an estate.

Donor — a person who grants a power of attorney.

Encumbrance — usually a mortgage or charge upon property securing the payment of a debt or other liability.

Enduring Power of Attorney — a power of attorney that remains in effect during the incapacity of the grantor.

Estate — all the property belonging to a person (at death, in Scotland).

Euthanasia — literally 'a good death', refers to the practice of taking active measures to end the suffering of a terminally ill patient.

Execute — to sign or otherwise complete the formalities of a legal document.

Executor (or **executrix**, if female) — a person nominated in a Testamentary Will to ensure that a testator's wishes are carried out and the Will followed.

E–I

Executor-dative — in Scotland, a person appointed by the Court (usually in the case of an intestacy) to manage the deceased's estate.

Executor-nominate — in Scotland, a person nominated in a Will to manage the deceased's estate.

General legacy — a gift of money or shares paid from the general assets of the estate.

General Power of Attorney — a power of attorney that is automatically annulled after the Donor becomes mentally incapable.

Grant of letters of administration — in England and Wales, the official document obtained by administrators of an estate on an administration intestacy showing that they have the legal authority to deal with the deceased's property.

Grant of letters of administration with Will annexed — in England and Wales, the official document obtained by administrators where there is a Will, but the executors named are unwilling or unable to act, showing they have the legal authority to deal with the deceased's property.

Grant of probate — in England and Wales, a court order giving an executor the legal right to deal with the deceased's assets.

Guardian — a person with legal control and responsibility for a minor child.

Health Care Proxy — in England and Wales, an individual appointed in a Living Will whom doctors may consult on a patient's health.

Informant — the person who registers the death.

Inheritance Tax — a tax imposed on a person's estate upon death and in some cases on gifts during the person's lifetime.

Insolvent estate — an estate where the debts of the deceased and other liabilities of the estate, including funeral and administration expenses, exceed the value of assets of the estate.

Intestacy rules — the rules which govern the distribution of property belonging to a person who dies intestate.

Intestate — the deceased is intestate if he or she dies without leaving a valid Will.

Issue — child, grandchild or more remote descendant including children born either within or outside marriage, and adopted children.

J–P

Joint property — property owned jointly with another person or persons.

Joint tenancy — in English law, a way of holding property jointly whereby when one of the joint owners dies, his or her share passes automatically to the other joint owner.

Legacy — usually a gift of money in a Will.

Legal rights — in Scotland, the claims which the surviving spouse and/or issue have to share in the deceased's estate whether or not the deceased died intestate.

Legatee — a person who receives a gift under a Will.

Letters of Administration — in English law, similar to Grant of Probate but used when there is a Will but no acting executors or there is no Will.

Life estate — an interest in an estate or income from a trust containing that estate that is limited to the life of the beneficiary.

Life interest — entitlement to income for life under a trust. When the person with a life interest dies, the property is not distributed in accordance with his or her Will or intestacy but is dealt with in accordance with the Will of the person who set up the trust.

Liferent — In Scottish law, a life interest.

Limited power — an authority that is restricted to specified acts or type of acts, or to a specified time period.

Minor — under English law, a person under the age of 18.

Mortgage — a loan secured on land.

Nominated property — property which the deceased has nominated a particular person to receive after his or her death (certain National Savings investments and government stock only).

Obtaining probate or obtaining Confirmation — the process of proving the validity of a Will and the executors' authority to manage the estate.

Pecuniary legacy — a gift of money in a Will.

Per stirpes — division between a number of beneficiaries according to the branches of the family as opposed to equally among all the beneficiaries.

Personal representatives — executors or administrators.

P–S

Power reserved letter — in England and Wales, a letter issued by the Probate Registry which an executor signs in order to renounce his or her duties as executor for the time being.

Public Guardian — in Scotland, the Government Officer appointed to deal with Continuing Powers of Attorney or Welfare Powers of Attorney.

Ratification — confirmation of an act or of the validity of an act.

Registered land — land or buildings, the ownership of which is registered at HM Land Registry.

Registration — the process through which in England and Wales an Enduring Power of Attorney is placed under the jurisdiction of the Court of Protection or in Scotland a Continuing Power of Attorney or Welfare Power of Attorney is placed under the jurisdiction of the Public Guardian.

Residuary beneficiary — a beneficiary who receives all or part of the residue of an estate.

Residuary gift — a gift of residue made in a Will.

Residuary legatee — a person who receives all or part of the residue of a person's estate.

Residue — the remainder of an estate after the deduction of tax, debts, specific gifts, legacies and the expenses of administration.

Resign — in Scotland, to refuse or renounce a right of authority.

Resuscitate — to revive or bring back to consciousness.

Revoke — to take back, withdraw or cancel.

Specific legacy or specific gift — a gift of a particular item of property in a Will.

Statute — an Act of Parliament.

Substitutional beneficiary — a person designated as a beneficiary in case another beneficiary predeceases you, fails to survive you for a specified period or fails to reach a specified age.

Survivorship clause — a clause in your Will stating what is to happen to your property on a failure of a nominated beneficiary to survive.

S–W

Survivorship destination — in Scotland, a way of holding property in joint names whereby when one of the joint owners dies his or her share passes automatically to the surviving joint owner(s).

Tenancy in common — in English law, a state of joint ownership in which each person owns a percentage of the property.

Testamentary Will — a legal document that sets out the wishes of the Testator for the distribution of his or her estate and certain other matters after his or her death.

Testator (or **testatrix**, if female) — a person who makes a Will.

Testing clause — the clause at the end of a Will declaring the date and place of signing and the names and designations of the witness or witnesses.

Title — ownership.

Trust — an arrangement under which a person or persons (the trustee or trustees) holds and manages property for the benefit of another person or persons (the trust beneficiary or beneficiaries).

Unregistered land — land or buildings, the ownership of which is not registered at HM Land Registry.

Witness — a person who signs a Will to verify the testator's signature on it.

Forms

This book contains examples of the following documents for reference when drawing up your own. You may obtain copies of these forms from the Law Pack P107 *Last Will & Testament* and P104 *Power of Attorney* Kits, your local Probate Registry or Sheriff Clerk's office, the Capital Taxes Office, or as indicated below.

Last Will & Testament forms

Power of Attorney forms (including Living Will)

Last Will & Testament forms

For England and Wales, refer to either England & Wales Will Form 1, 2 or 3 depending on your circumstances and requirements. This depends upon whom you wish to receive the residue of your estate.

- Example *Will Form 1* should be used if you want to give the residue of your estate to an adult and provide for another adult to take instead if the first fails to survive you by 28 days.

- Example *Will Form 2* should be used if you want to give the residue of your estate to an adult and provide for your children to take instead in equal shares if the adult fails to survive you by 28 days.

- Example *Will Form 3* should be used if you want to give the residue of your estate to your children in equal shares in any event.

For Scotland, refer to either Scotland Will Form 1, 2 or 3 depending on your circumstances and requirements. This depends upon whom you wish to receive the residue of your estate.

- Example *Will Form 1* should be used if you want to give the residue of your estate to an adult and provide for another adult to take instead if the first fails to survive you by 28 days.

- Example *Will Form 2* should be used if you want to give the residue of your estate to an adult and provide for your children to take instead in equal shares if the adult fails to survive you by 28 days.

- Example *Will Form 3* should be used if you want to give the residue of your estate to your children in equal shares in any event.

Last Will & Testament

ENGLAND & WALES WILL FORM 1 - RESIDUE TO ADULT

PRINT NAME AND ADDRESS

THIS Last Will & Testament is made by me RICHARD BERNARD ROSS

of 28 Stapleforth Road, London SW6 4LJ

I REVOKE all previous wills and codicils.

EXECUTORS' NAMES AND ADDRESSES

I APPOINT as executors and trustees of my will

DAVID PETER ROSS and ANTHONY WILLIAMS

of 5 Maple Terrace of 17 St. George's Crescent

London SW10 2PZ Reading RG7 9XY

SUBSTITUTIONAL EXECUTOR'S NAME AND ADDRESS

and should one or more of them fail to or be unable to act I APPOINT to fill any vacancy

GILLIAN ROSS

of 5 Maple Terrace, London SW10 2PZ

SPECIFIC GIFTS AND LEGACIES

I GIVE My cottage in St. Ives, Cornwall, to my brother, DAVID PETER ROSS, free from all encumbrances.

One thousand pounds to my friend, ANTHONY WILLIAMS.

RESIDUARY GIFT

I GIVE the residue of my estate to DAVID PETER ROSS, SUSANNA HILL and NIGEL JONES in equal shares

but if he/she or (if I have indicated more than one person) any of them fails to survive me by 28 days or if this gift or any part of it fails for any other reason, then I GIVE the residue of my estate or the part of it affected to

the other residuary beneficiaries in proportion to their shares.

FUNERAL WISHES

I WISH my body to be ☑ buried ☐ cremated other instructions at St. Dunstans Old Church, London SW6

DATE

SIGNED by the above-named testator in our presence on the 10th day of October 20 03 and then by us in the testator's presence

TESTATOR'S SIGNATURE

SIGNED *Richard Ross*

WITNESSES' SIGNATURES NAMES AND ADDRESSES

SIGNED *Mary Tucker* SIGNED *S. Knox*

MARY TUCKER SIMON KNOX

of 14 Ravenscroft Gardens of 86 Preston Square

London N12 5TB London SW6

occupation Teacher occupation Computer Consultant

LAST WILL & TESTAMENT

ENGLAND & WALES WILL FORM 2 - RESIDUE TO AN ADULT BUT IF HE/SHE DIES TO CHILDREN

PRINT NAME AND ADDRESS

THIS Last Will & Testament is made by me   GILLIAN ROSS

of   5 Maple Terrace, London SW10 2PZ

I REVOKE all previous wills and codicils.

EXECUTORS' NAMES AND ADDRESSES

I APPOINT as executors and trustees of my will

DAVID PETER ROSS   and   THERESA MUNDY

of   5 Maple Terrace   of   9 Kings Walk

London SW10 2PZ   Leamington Spa LM9 4BL

SUBSTITUTIONAL EXECUTOR'S NAME AND ADDRESS

and should one or more of them fail to or be unable to act I APPOINT to fill any vacancy

THOMAS WAITE

of   36 Amber Road, London SW3 5HM

GUARDIAN'S NAME AND ADDRESS

I APPOINT   THERESA MUNDY

of   9 Kings Walk, Leamington Spa LM9 4BL

to be guardian of any of my children who are minors if my husband/wife dies before me.

SPECIFIC GIFTS AND LEGACIES

I GIVE All of my jewellery to my daughter MARY JANE ROSS.

£1,000 to each of my sons, JAMES ROSS and ALEXANDER GUY ROSS.

My motor car, registration number P488 YVV, to my friend PETER HARRISON.

RESIDUARY GIFT

I GIVE the rest of my estate to my executors and trustees to hold on trust to pay my debts, taxes and testamentary expenses and pay the residue to

my husband DAVID PETER ROSS

but if he/she or (if I have indicated more than one person) any of them fails to survive me by 28 days or if this gift or any part of it fails for any other reason, then I GIVE the residue of my estate or the part of it affected to those of my children who survive me and attain the age of __21__ years if more than one in equal shares

(insert age at which you want your children to inherit capital)

PROVIDED THAT if any of my children dies before me or after me but under that age, I GIVE the share that child would have taken to his or her own children who attain 18 equally. If no person shall inherit the residue of my estate or part of it under the preceding gifts, I GIVE it to

THERESA MUNDY

TRUSTEES' POWERS

WHILE a child is a minor, my trustees may at their absolute discretion use all or any part of the income from the child's share for the child's maintenance, education or benefit.

FUNERAL WISHES

I WISH my body to be ☐ buried ☑ cremated other instructions _____

DATE

SIGNED by the above-named testator in our presence on the __10th__ day of __October__ 20 __03__ and then by us in the testator's presence

TESTATOR'S SIGNATURE

SIGNED *Gillian Ross*

WITNESSES' SIGNATURES NAMES AND ADDRESSES

SIGNED *Ruth Grant*   SIGNED *Jane Paxford*

RUTH GRANT   JANE PAXFORD

of   90 Dorset Mansions   of   32 Church Grove

London W14 2BS   London SW6 6RQ

occupation Housewife   occupation Receptionist

LAST WILL & TESTAMENT

ENGLAND & WALES WILL FORM 3 - RESIDUE DIRECT TO CHILDREN

PRINT NAME AND ADDRESS

THIS Last Will & Testament is made by me   GILLIAN ROSS

of   5 Maple Terrace, London SW10 2PZ

I REVOKE all previous wills and codicils.

EXECUTORS' NAMES AND ADDRESSES

I APPOINT as executors and trustees of my will

DAVID PETER ROSS   and   THERESA MUNDY

of   5 Maple Terrace   of   9 Kings Walk

London SW10 2PZ   Leamington Spa LM9 4BL

SUBSTITUTIONAL EXECUTOR'S NAME AND ADDRESS

and should one or more of them fail to or be unable to act I APPOINT to fill any vacancy

THOMAS WAITE

of   36 Amber Road, London SW3 5HM

GUARDIAN'S NAME AND ADDRESS

I APPOINT   THERESA MUNDY

of   9 Kings Walk, Leamington Spa LM9 4BL

to be guardian of any of my children who are minors if my husband/wife dies before me.

SPECIFIC GIFTS AND LEGACIES

I GIVE   All of my jewellery to my daughter MARY JANE ROSS.

£1,000 to each of my sons, JAMES ROSS and ALEXANDER GUY ROSS.

My house at 5 Maple Terrace London SW10 2PZ to my husband

DAVID PETER ROSS subject to the mortgage on it.

RESIDUARY GIFT (insert age at which you want your children to inherit capital)

I GIVE the rest of my estate to my executors and trustees to hold on trust to pay my debts, taxes and testamentary expenses and pay the residue to those of my children who survive me and attain the age of __21__ years if more than one in equal shares PROVIDED THAT if any of my children dies before me or after me but under that age, I GIVE the share that child would have taken to his or her own children who attain 18 equally. If no person shall inherit the residue of my estate under the preceding gifts, I GIVE it to

THERESA MUNDY

TRUSTEES' POWERS

WHILE a child is a minor, my trustees may at their absolute discretion use all or any part of the income from the child's share for the child's maintenance, education or benefit.

FUNERAL WISHES

I WISH my body to be   ☐ buried   ☑ cremated   other instructions _____

DATE

SIGNED by the above-named testator in our presence on the __10th__ day of __October__ 20 __03__ and then by us in the testator's presence

TESTATOR'S SIGNATURE

SIGNED   *Gillian Ross*

WITNESSES' SIGNATURES NAMES AND ADDRESSES

SIGNED   *Ruth Grant*   SIGNED   *Jane Paxford*

RUTH GRANT   JANE PAXFORD

of   90 Dorset Mansions   of   32 Church Grove

London W14 2BS   London SW6 6RQ

occupation Housewife   occupation Receptionist

𝕷ast 𝖂ill & 𝕿estament

SCOTLAND WILL FORM 1 - RESIDUE TO ADULT

PRINT FULL NAME AND ADDRESS

THIS Last Will & Testament is made by me   RICHARD BERNARD ROSS

of   28 Stapleforth Road, Edinburgh EH22 4LJ

I REVOKE all previous wills and codicils.

EXECUTORS' FULL NAMES AND ADDRESSES

I APPOINT as executors and trustees of my will

name   DAVID PETER ROSS   and name ANTHONY WILLIAMS

of   5 Maple Terrace   of 17 St George⬚s Crescent

             Edinburgh EH10 2PZ   Aberdeen AB7 9XY

SUBSTITUTIONAL EXECUTOR'S FULL NAME AND ADDRESS

and should one or more of them fail to or be unable to act I APPOINT to fill any vacancy

name   GILLIAN ROSS

of   5 Maple Terrace, Edinburgh EH10 2PZ

DEBTS AND FUNERAL EXPENSES

I direct my executors to settle my debts and funeral expenses and the expenses of administering my estate;

SPECIFIC GIFTS AND PECUNIARY LEGACIES

I GIVE   My cottage in St Andrews, Fife, to my brother, DAVID

PETER ROSS, residing at 10 South Street, Dundee, free from all

encumbrances.

          One thousand pounds to my friend, ANTHONY WILLIAMS,

residing at 3 Forest Avenue, St Andrews.

Richard B Ross

(Testator's signature)

RESIDUARY GIFT   I GIVE the residue of my estate to   DAVID PETER ROSS, SUSANNA HILL and NIGEL

JONES in equal shares

but if he/she or (if I have indicated more than one person) any of them fails to survive me by 28 days or if this gift or any part of it fails for any other reason, then I GIVE the residue of my estate or the part of it affected to

the other residuary beneficiaries in proportion to their shares.

EXECUTORS' POWERS   And my executors shall have all the powers of gratuitous trustees;

With reference to these presents I HEREBY DECLARE as follows, videlicet:-

That all pecuniary legacies shall be payable without interest and within six months of the date of my death;

That all specific bequests shall be subject to the beneficiary paying the delivery costs;

FUNERAL WISHES   I WISH my body to be ☑ buried ☐ cremated ☐ other instructions   At St Dunstans Old

Church, Edinburgh

And in the event of my death, (not survived by my wife/husband),

GUARDIAN'S FULL   I NOMINATE and APPOINT
NAME AND ADDRESS   of

to be guardian to such of my children as are under the age of full legal capacity at my death;

DATE   IN WITNESS WHEREOF these presents written on this and the preceding page are subscribed by me at

address 28 Stapleforth Rd Edinburgh EH10 2PZ on the 7th day of January

Two Thousand and Three_____ before this witness:-

TESTATOR'S   SIGNED   *Richard B Ross*
SIGNATURE

WITNESS'S   SIGNED   *Ruth Grant*
SIGNATURE

WITNESS'S FULL   name   RUTH ELIZABETH GRANT
NAME AND ADDRESS   of   90 Weir Mansions

Edinburgh EH12 2BS

occupation Housewife

ℒAST 𝔚ILL & 𝔗ESTAMENT

SCOTLAND WILL FORM 2 - RESIDUE TO AN ADULT BUT IF HE/SHE DIES TO CHILDREN

PRINT FULL NAME AND ADDRESS

THIS Last Will and Testament is made by me   GILLIAN ROSS

of   5 Maple Terrace, Edinburgh EH10 2PZ

I REVOKE all previous wills and codicils.

EXECUTORS' FULL NAMES AND ADDRESSES

I APPOINT as executors and trustees of my will

name   DAVID PETER ROSS   and   name   THERESA MUNDY

of   5 Maple Terrace   of   9 King's Walk

            Edinburgh EH10 2PZ   Glasgow G9 4BL

SUBSTITUTIONAL EXECUTOR'S FULL NAME AND ADDRESS

and should one or more of them fail to or be unable to act I APPOINT to fill any vacancy

name   THOMAS JAMES WAITE

of   36 Amber Road, Edinburgh EH3 5HM

DEBTS AND FUNERAL EXPENSES

I direct my executors and trustees to settle my debts and funeral expenses and the expenses of administering my estate;

SPECIFIC GIFTS AND PECUNIARY LEGACIES

I GIVE   All of my jewellery to my daughter, MARY JANE ROSS, residing at 5 Maple Terrace

Edinburgh EH10 2PZ.

One thousand pounds to each of my sons, JAMES TARQUIN ROSS and ALEXANDER ROSS,

both residing at 5 Maple Terrace, Edinburgh EH10 2PZ.

My motor car, registration number K288 YVV, to my friend, PETER HARRISON, residing at

24 West Street, Perth.

RESIDUARY GIFT

I GIVE the residue of my estate to my husband DAVID PETER ROSS.

but if he/she or (if I have indicated more than one person) any of them fails to survive me by 28 days or if this gift or any part of it fails for any other reason, then I direct my trustees to pay, convey and make over the said residue so far as not disposed of equally between or among or wholly to such of my children as survive the coming into

(insert age at which you want your children to inherit capital)

operation of this Clause, and have then attained or thereafter attain the age of ___21___ years complete, along with the issue who do so survive and attain the said age of any of my children who may fail to so survive or do so survive but fail to attain the said age, such issue taking equally between or among them "per stirpes" if more than one the share of residue, original and accrescing, such as the parent would have taken on survivance;

Gillian Ross

(Testator's signature)

TRUSTEES' POWERS
(insert age at which you want your children to inherit capital)

DECLARING that during the minority of any beneficiary hereunder (which for this purpose shall be while such beneficiary is under the age of __21__ years complete) who is prospectively entitled to a share of the capital of the said residue in terms of this Clause, my trustees shall apply so much, if any, of the income of the share of capital to which he or she is for the time being prospectively entitled as they in their absolute discretion may from time to time consider to be necessary for his or her maintenance, education or benefit and my trustees shall accumulate so much of the said income as is not applied for the foregoing purposes and add the same to the capital of such share; and

(insert age at which you want your children to become entitled to receive the income)

That on the attainment of the age of __18__ years complete of any beneficiary hereunder who is prospectively entitled to a share of the capital of the said residue, my trustees shall, until he or she becomes entitled to receive the said capital, pay to him or her the whole income of the said capital to which he or she is for the time being prospectively entitled and the whole income of any accumulations thereon; and

With reference to these presents I HEREBY DECLARE as follows, videlicet:-

That all pecuniary legacies shall be payable without interest and within six months of the date of my death;

That all specific bequests shall be subject to the beneficiary paying the delivery costs;

That no beneficiary shall take a vested interest in any part of the said residue until the term or terms of payment thereof except that all payments or advances which may be made by my trustees by virtue of the powers herein conferred on them shall vest in the beneficiary receiving the same at the date of payment or advance;

That my trustees shall have power in their absolute discretion to advance to any residuary beneficiary hereunder, any part or even the whole of his or her prospective share of the said residue for any purpose which my trustees shall deem to be for his or her permanent advantage or benefit and on such terms and conditions, as my trustees in their uncontrolled discretion think fit;

That my trustees shall have power to pay and make over in whole or in part any funds due or advanced to or on account of any beneficiary under the age of full legal capacity to his or her legal guardian, the receipt of such guardian constituting a sufficient discharge;

That there shall be no apportionment of income between capital and revenue on any occasion, all income being deemed to have accrued at the date upon which it is payable;

And I PROVIDE and DECLARE that my trustees shall have all the powers and immunities of gratuitous trustees and shall not be restricted to investments authorised by the Trustee Investments Act 1961;

FUNERAL WISHES

I WISH my body to be ☐ buried ☑ cremated ☐ other instructions _____

And in the event of my death, (not survived by my wife/husband),

GUARDIAN'S FULL NAME AND ADDRESS

I NOMINATE AND APPOINT   Theresa Mundy

of 9 King☐s Walk, Glasgow G9 4BL

to be the guardian to such of my children as are under the age of full legal capacity at my death;

DATE

IN WITNESS WHEREOF these presents written on this and the preceding page are subscribed by me at

address 5 Maple Terrace Edinburgh EH10 2PZ on the 10th day of January

Two Thousand and Three _____ before this witness:-

TESTATOR'S SIGNATURE

SIGNED   *Gillian Ross*

WITNESS'S SIGNATURE

SIGNED   *Ruth Grant*

WITNESS'S FULL NAME AND ADDRESS

name   RUTH ELIZABETH GRANT

of   90 Weir Mansions

          Edinburgh EH12 2BS

occupation Housewife

ℒast 𝔚ill & 𝔗estament

SCOTLAND WILL FORM 3 - RESIDUE DIRECT TO CHILDREN

PRINT FULL NAME AND ADDRESS

THIS Last Will and Testament is made by me   GILLIAN ROSS

of   5 Maple Terrace, Edinburgh, EH10 2PZ

I REVOKE all previous wills and codicils.

EXECUTORS' FULL NAMES AND ADDRESSES

I APPOINT as executors and trustees of my will

name   DAVID PETER ROSS   and   name   THERESA MUNDY

of   5 Maple Terrace   of   9 King□s Walk

        Edinburgh EH10 2PZ   Glasgow G9 4BL

SUBSTITUTIONAL EXECUTOR'S FULL NAME AND ADDRESS

and should one or more of them fail to or be unable to act I APPOINT to fill any vacancy

name   THOMAS JAMES WAITE

of   36 Amber Road, Edinburgh EH3 5HM

DEBTS AND FUNERAL EXPENSES

I direct my executors and trustees to settle my debts and funeral expenses and the expenses of administering my estate;

SPECIFIC GIFTS AND PECUNIARY LEGACIES

I GIVE   All of my jewellery to my daughter MARY JANE ROSS

residing at 5 Maple Terrace Edinburgh EH10 2PZ.

One thousand pounds to each of my sons, JAMES TARQUIN

ROSS and ALEXANDER GUY ROSS, both residing at 5 Maple

Terrace, Edinburgh EH10 2PZ.

My house at 5 Maple Terrace Edinburgh EH10 2PZ to my

husband, DAVID PETER ROSS, subject to the mortgage on it.

RESIDUARY GIFT

(insert age at which you want your children to inherit capital)

I direct my trustees to pay, convey and make over the residue of my estate equally between or among or wholly to such of my children as survive the coming into operation of this Clause, and have then attained or thereafter attain the age of   21   years complete, along with the issue who do so survive and attain the said age of any of my children who may fail to so survive or do so survive but fail to attain the said age, such issue taking equally between or among them "per stirpes" if more than one the share of residue, original and accrescing, such as the parent would have taken on survivance;

Gillian Ross
_____
(Testator's signature)

TRUSTEES' POWERS
(insert age at which you
want your children to
inherit capital)

DECLARING that during the minority of any beneficiary hereunder (which for this purpose shall be while such beneficiary is under the age of _21_ years complete) who is prospectively entitled to a share of the capital of the said residue in terms of this Clause, my trustees shall apply so much, if any, of the income of the share of capital to which he or she is for the time being prospectively entitled as they in their absolute discretion may from time to time consider to be necessary for his or her maintenance, education or benefit and my trustees shall accumulate so much of the said income as is not applied for the foregoing purposes and add the same to the capital of such share; and

(insert age at which you
want your children to
become entitled to
receive the income)

That on the attainment of the age of _18_ years complete of any beneficiary hereunder who is prospectively entitled to a share of the capital of the said residue, my trustees shall, until he or she becomes entitled to receive the said capital, pay to him or her the whole income of the said capital to which he or she is for the time being prospectively entitled and the whole income of any accumulations thereon; and

With reference to these presents I HEREBY DECLARE as follows, videlicet:-

That all pecuniary legacies shall be payable without interest and within six months of the date of my death;

That all specific bequests shall be subject to the beneficiary paying the delivery costs;

That no beneficiary shall take a vested interest in any part of the said residue until the term or terms of payment thereof except that all payments or advances which may be made by my trustees by virtue of the powers herein conferred on them shall vest in the beneficiary receiving the same at the date of payment or advance;

That my trustees shall have power in their absolute discretion to advance to any residuary beneficiary hereunder, any part or even the whole of his or her prospective share of the said residue for any purpose which my trustees shall deem to be for his or her permanent advantage or benefit and on such terms and conditions, as my trustees in their uncontrolled discretion think fit;

That my trustees shall have power to pay and make over in whole or in part any funds due or advanced to or on account of any beneficiary under the age of full legal capacity to his or her legal guardian, the receipt of such guardian constituting a sufficient discharge.

That there shall be no apportionment of income between capital and revenue on any occasion, all income being deemed to have accrued at the date upon which it is payable;

And I PROVIDE and DECLARE that my trustees shall have all the powers and immunities of gratuitous trustees and shall not be restricted to investments authorised by the Trustee Investments Act 1961;

FUNERAL WISHES

I WISH my body to be ☐ buried ☑ cremated ☐ other instructions _____

_____

And in the event of my death, (not survived by my wife/husband),

GUARDIAN'S FULL
NAME AND ADDRESS

I NOMINATE AND APPOINT   Theresa Mundy

of 9 King□s Walk, Glasgow G9 4BL

to be guardian to such of my children as are under the age of full legal capacity at my death;

DATE

IN WITNESS WHEREOF these presents written on this and the preceding page are subscribed by me at

address 5 Maple Terrace Edinburgh EH10 2PZ on the 10th day of   January

Two Thousand and Three_____ before this witness:-

TESTATOR'S
SIGNATURE

SIGNED   *Gillian Ross*

WITNESS'S
SIGNATURE

SIGNED   *Ruth Grant*

WITNESS'S FULL
NAME AND ADDRESS

name   RUTH ELIZABETH GRANT

of   90 Weir Mansions

             Edinburgh EH12 2BS

occupation Housewife

FORM OF LETTER TO EXECUTOR

Dear ____DAVID_____

I am writing to confirm that I have named you as executor of my Will, dated

____10/10_____ year _03_ .

- A copy of my Will is enclosed.

- My signed original will has been lodged with __MY SOLICITOR_____ .

- I have named _ANTHONY WILLIAMS__ as a co-executor.*

- My solicitor is __ROBERT SMITH____ at _SHERMAN SOLICITORS_ *

Please confirm to me in writing that you are willing to act as my executor.

Yours sincerely

Richard Ross

* delete as necessary

[Warning: do not include any other instructions to your executors in this letter.]

Enduring Power of Attorney

ENDURING POWER OF ATTORNEY

Part A: About using this form

1. **You may choose one attorney or more than one.** If you choose one attorney then you must delete everything between the square brackets on the first page of the form. If you choose more than one, you must decide whether they are able to act:
   - Jointly (that is, they must all act together and cannot act separately) or
   - Jointly and severally (that is, they can all act together but they can also act separately if they wish).

   On the first page of the form, show what you have decided by crossing out one of the alternatives.

2. **If you give your attorney(s) general power** in relation to all your property and affairs, it means that they will be able to deal with your money or property and may be able to sell your house.

3. **If you don't want your attorney(s) to have such wide powers**, you can include any restrictions you like. For example, you can include a restriction that your attorney(s) must not act on your behalf until they have reason to believe that you are becoming mentally incapable; or a restriction as to what your attorney(s) may do. Any restrictions you choose must be written or typed where indicated on the second page of the form.

4. **If you are a trustee** (and please remember that co-ownership of a home involves trusteeship), you should seek legal advice if you want your attorney(s) to act as a trustee on your behalf.

5. **Unless you put in a restriction preventing it** your attorney(s) will be able to use any of your money or property to make any provision which you yourself might be expected to make for their own needs or the needs of other people. Your attorney(s) will also be able to use your money to make gifts, but only for reasonable amounts in relation to the value of your money and property.

6. **Your attorney(s) can recover the out-of-pocket expenses** of acting as your attorney(s). If your attorney(s) are professional people, for example solicitors or accountants, they may be able to charge for their professional services as well. You may wish to provide expressly for remuneration of your attorney(s) (although if they are trustees they may not be allowed to accept it).

7. **If your attorney(s) have reason to believe** that you have become or are becoming mentally incapable of managing your affairs, your attorney(s) will have to apply to the Court of Protection for registration of this power.

8. **Before applying to the Court of Protection for registration** of this power, your attorney(s) must give written notice that that is what they are going to do, to you and your nearest relatives as defined in the Enduring Powers of Attorney Act 1985. You or your relatives will be able to object if you or they disagree with registration.

9. **This is a simplified explanation** of what the Enduring Powers of Attorney Act 1985 and the Rules and Regulations say. If you need more guidance, you or your advisers will need to look at the Act itself and the Rules and Regulations. The Rules are the Court of Protection (Enduring Powers of Attorney) Rules 1986 (Statutory Instrument 1986 No. 127). The Regulations are the Enduring Powers of Attorney (Prescribed Form) Regulations 1990 (Statutory Instrument 1990 No. 1376).

10. **Note to Attorney(s)**
    After the power has been registered you should notify the Court of Protection if the donor dies or recovers.

11. **Note to Donor**
    Some of these explanatory notes may not apply to the form you are using if it has already been adapted to suit your particular requirements.

YOU CAN CANCEL THIS POWER AT ANY TIME BEFORE IT HAS TO BE REGISTERED

Part B: To be completed by the donor ' (the person appointing the attorney(s))

Dont sign this form unless you understand what it means

Please read the notes in the margin which follow and which are part of the form itself.
Donor's name and address.

I ___DAVID PETER ROSS___

of ___5 MAPLE TERRACE, LONDON, SW10 2PZ___

Donor's date of birth.

born on ___20/06/30___

appoint ___MRS GILLIAN ROSS___

of ___5 MAPLE TERRACE, LONDON, SW10 2PZ___

See note 1 on the front of this form. If you are appointing only one attorney you should cross out everything between the square brackets. If appointing more than two attorneys please give the additional name(s) on an attached sheet.

● [and _____

~~of~~ _____

Cross out the one which does not apply (see note 1 on the front of this form).

● ~~jointly~~
● ~~jointly and severally]~~

to be my attorney(s) for the purpose of the Enduring Powers of Attorney Act 1985

Cross out the one which does not apply (see note 2 on the front of this form). Add any additional powers.

● with general authority to act on my behalf
● ~~with authority to do the following on my behalf:~~

If you don't want the attorney(s) to have general power, you must give details here of what authority you are giving the attorney(s).

in relation to

Cross out the one which does not apply.

● all my property and affairs
● ~~the following property and affairs:~~

Part B: continued

Please read the notes in the margin which follow and which are part of the form itself.
If there are restrictions or conditions, insert them here; if not, cross out these words if you wish (see note 3 on the front of this form).

● ~~subject to the following restrictions and conditions:~~

I intend that this power shall continue even if I become mentally incapable.

I have read or have had read to me the notes in Part A which are part of, and explain, this form.

If this form is being signed at your direction: —

● the person signing must not be an attorney or any witness (to Parts B or C);
● you must add a statement that this form has been signed at your direction;
● a second witness is necessary (please see below).

Your signature (or mark).

Signed by me as a deed *David P Ross*
and delivered

Date.

on   10TH APRIL 2003

Someone must witness your signature.

Signature of witness.

in the presence of   *Thomas Waite*

Full name of witness   THOMAS WAITE

Your attorney(s) cannot be your witness. It is not advisable for your husband or wife to be your witness.

Address of witness   36 AMBER ROAD

LONDON SW3 5HM

A second witness is only necessary if this form is not being signed by you personally but at your direction (for example, if a physical disability prevents you from signing).

Signature of second witness.

in the presence of _____

Full name of witness _____

Address of witness _____

Part C: To be completed by the attorney(s)

Note 1. This form may be adapted to provide for execution by a corporation.
  2. If there is more than one attorney additional sheets in the form as shown below must be added to this Part C.

Please read the notes in the margin which follow and which are part of the form itself.

Don't sign this form before the donor has signed Part B or if, in your opinion, the donor was already mentally incapable at the time of signing Part B.

If this form is being signed at your direction: —
- the person signing must not be an attorney or any witness (to Parts B or C);
- you must add a statement that this form has been signed at your direction;
- a second witness is necessary (please see below).

Signature (or mark) of attorney.

Date.

Signature of witness.

The attorney must sign the form and his signature must be witnessed. The donor may not be the witness and one attorney may not witness the signature of the other.

I understand that I have a duty to apply to the Court for the registration of this form under the Enduring Powers of Attorney Act 1985 when the donor is becoming or has become mentally incapable.

I also understand my limited power to use the donor's property to benefit persons other than the donor.

I am not a minor

Signed by me as a deed and delivered   *Gillian Ross*

on   10TH APRIL 2003

in the presence of   *Thomas Waite*

Full name of witness   THOMAS WAITE

Address of witness   36 AMBER ROAD

LONDON SW3 5HM

A second witness is only necessary if this form is not being signed by you personally but at your direction (for example, if a physical disability prevents you from signing).
Signature of second witness.

in the presence of

Full name of witness

Address of witness

Reproduced by Law Pack Publishing Ltd with the permission of the Controller of HMSO

SCHEDULE 1
Form EP1
Court of Protection
Enduring Powers of Attorney Act

Notice of intention to apply for registration

To ....

of ....

TAKE NOTICE THAT

> *This form may be adapted for use by three or more attorneys.*

I .....MRS GILLIAN ROSS..

of ....5 MAPLE TERRACE, LONDON, SW10 2PZ...............

and I ....

of ....

> *Give the name and address of the donor*

the attorney(s) of .....DAVID PETER ROSS.........................

............10TH APRIL 2003...

of .....5 MAPLE TERRACE, LONDON, SW10 2PZ...............

....

intend to apply to the Public Trustee for registration of the enduring power

of attorney appointing me (us) attorney(s) and made by the donor on

the ....

> *It will be necessary for you to produce evidence in support of your objection.*
> *If evidence is available please send it with your objection, the attorney(s) will be given an opportunity to respond to your objection.*

1. If you wish to object to the proposed registration you have 4 weeks from the day on which this notice is given to you to do so in writing. Any objections should be sent to the Public Trustee and should contain the following details:

   - your name and address;

   - any relationship to the donor;

   - if you are not the donor, the name and address of the donor;

   - the name and address of the attorney;

   - the grounds for objecting to the registration of the enduring power.

> *The grounds upon which you can object are limited and are shown at 2 overleaf.*

EP1

Note. The instrument means the enduring power of attorney made by the donor which it is sought to register.

2. The grounds on which you may object are:

- that the power purported to have been created by the instrument is not valid as an enduring power of attorney;

- that the power created by the instrument no longer subsists;

- that the application is premature because the donor is not yet becoming mentally incapable;

- that fraud or undue pressure was used to induce the donor to make the power;

The attorney(s) does not have to be a relative. Relatives are not entitled to know of the existence of the enduring power of attorney prior to being given this notice.

- that the attorney is unsuitable to be the donor's attorney (having regard to all the circumstances and in particular the attorney's relationship to or connection with the donor).

Note. This is addressed only to the donor.

3. You are informed that while the enduring power of attorney remains registered, you will not be able to revoke it until the Court of Protection confirms the revocation.

Note. This notice should be signed by every one of the attorneys who are applying to register the enduring power of attorney.

Signed *Gillian Ross* ....Dated 13TH JUNE 2003

Signed .... Dated ....

EP1

Court of Protection
Enduring Powers of Attorney Act 1985
Application for Registration

EP2

IMPORTANT: Please complete the form in <u>BLOCK CAPITALS</u> using a <u>black ballpoint pen</u>. For circled options please completely fill-in the appropriate choice.

Part One - The Donor

Please state the full name and present address of the donor. State the donor's first name in 'Forename 1' and the donor's other forenames/initials in 'Other Forenames'. If the donor's address on the enduring power of attorney is different give that one too. If necessary, complete several parts of the address on each Address line shown.

Mr ⊙   Mrs ○   Ms ○   Miss ○   Other ○   If Other, please specify here:

Last Name: R O S S

Forename 1: D A V I D

Other Forenames: P E T E R

Address 1: 5   M A P L E   T E R R A C E

Address 2:

Address 3:

Town/City: L O N D O N

County:

Postcode: S W 1 0   2 P Z

Address on the enduring power of attorney (if different from above) :

Address 1:

Address 2:

Town/City:

County: Postcode:

You can find the donor's date of birth in Part B of the enduring power of attorney.

Donor Date of Birth: 2 0 | 0 6 | 1 9 3 0
D D   M M   Y Y Y Y

If the exact date is unknown please state the year of birth

Part Two - Attorney One

Please state the full name and present address of the attorney. If applicable, include the Company Name in 'Address 1'

Mr ○   Mrs ⊙   Ms ○   Miss ○   Other ○   If Other, please specify here:

Last Name: R O S S

Forename 1: G I L L I A N

Other Forenames:

Continued overleaf

Part Two - Attorney One cont'd

Address 1: `5` `M` `A` `P` `L` `E` | `T` `E` `R` `R` `A` `C` `E`

Address 2:

Address 3:

Town/City: `L` `O` `N` `D` `O` `N`

County:

Postcode: `S` `W` `1` `0` | `2` `P` `Z`   DX No. (solicitors only):

DX Exchange (solicitors only):

Attorney Date of Birth: `2` `4` | `1` `0` | `1` `9` `3` `2`   Occupation: *INTERIOR DESIGNER*
D D   M M   Y Y Y Y

Daytime Tel No.: (STD Code): `0` `2` `0` `7` | `1` `2` `3` `4` `5` `6` `7`

Email Address: *GILROSS@LAWPACK.CO.UK*

Relationship to donor:
Spouse ☑   Child ○   Other Relation ○   No Relation ○   Solicitor ○   Other Professional ○

If 'Other Relation' or 'Other Professional', specify relationship:

Part B of the enduring power of attorney states whether the attorney is to act jointly, jointly and severally, or alone.

Appointment *(please fill the appropriate circle)*:   Jointly ○   Jointly and Severally ○   Alone ☑

Part Three - Attorney Two

Please state the full name and present address of the second attorney. If applicable, include the Company Name in 'Address 1'.

Mr ○   Mrs ○   Ms ○   Miss ○   Other ○   If Other, please specify here:

Last Name:

Forename 1:

Other Forenames:

Address 1:

Address 2:

Address 3:

Town/City:

County:

Postcode: DX No. (solicitors only):

DX Exchange (solicitors only):

Page 3 of 6

Part Three - Attorney Two cont'd

Attorney Date of Birth: ☐☐ ☐☐ ☐☐☐☐
D D M M Y Y Y Y

Occupation: ☐

Daytime Tel No.: ☐

Email Address: ☐

Relationship to donor:

Spouse	Child	Other Relation	No Relation	Solicitor	Other Professional
○	○	○	○	○	○

If 'Other Relation' or 'Other Professional', specify relationship: ☐

Part Four - Attorney Three

Please state the full name and present address of the third attorney.
If applicable, include the Company Name in 'Address 1'.

Mr ○ Mrs ○ Ms ○ Miss ○ Other ○

If Other, please specify here: ☐

Last Name: ☐

Forename 1: ☐

Other Forenames: ☐

Address 1: ☐

Address 2: ☐

Address 3: ☐

Town/City: ☐

County: ☐

Postcode: ☐

DX No. (solicitors only): ☐

DX Exchange (solicitors only): ☐

Attorney Date of Birth: ☐☐ ☐☐ ☐☐☐☐
D D M M Y Y Y Y

Occupation: ☐

Daytime Tel No.: ☐

Email Address: ☐

Relationship to donor:

Spouse	Child	Other Relation	No Relation	Solicitor	Other Professional
○	○	○	○	○	○

If 'Other Relation' or 'Other Professional', specify relationship: ☐

If there are additional attorneys, please complete the above details in the 'Additional Information' section (at the end of this form).

Part Five - The Enduring Power of Attorney

The date is the date that the donor signed the enduring power of attorney.
You can find this in Part B of the enduring power of attorney.

I (We) the attorney(s) apply to register the enduring power of attorney made by the donor under the above Act, the original of which accompanies this application.

~~I (We) have reason to believe that the donor is or is becoming mentally incapable.~~

Date of enduring power of attorney: `1 0` `0 4` `2 0 0 3`
D D   M M   Y Y Y Y

To your knowledge, has the donor made any other enduring power of attorney?: Yes ○   No ☑

If 'Yes', please give details below including registration date if applicable:

Part Six - Notice of Application to Donor

Notice must be given personally to the donor. It should be made clear if someone other than the attorney(s) gives the notice.

I (We) have given notice of the application to register in the prescribed form (EP1) to the donor personally.

If someone other than the attorney gives notice to the donor please complete the name, address and date details below:

Full Name:
Address 1:
Address 2:
Town/City:
County: Postcode:

On this date:
D D   M M   Y Y Y Y

Part Seven - Notice of Application to Relatives

If there are no relatives entitled to notice please ensure that the circle is filled below.

Please fill-in the circle if no relatives are entitled to notice: ☑

I (We) have given notice to register in the prescribed form (EP1) to the following relatives of the donor:

Name	Relationship to Donor	Address	Date notice given:
			D D M M Y Y Y Y

Name	Relationship to Donor	Address	Date notice given:
			D D M M Y Y Y Y

Name	Relationship to Donor	Address	Date notice given:
			D D M M Y Y Y Y

Name	Relationship to Donor	Address	Date notice given:
			D D M M Y Y Y Y

Continued overleaf

Part Seven - Notice of Application to Relatives cont'd

If there are additional relatives please complete the Relative Name, Relationship, Address and Date details in the 'Additional Information' section (at the end of this form).

Name	Relationship to Donor	Address

Date notice given:

D D   M M   Y Y Y Y

Part Eight - Notice of Application to Co-Attorney(s)

Do not complete this section if it does not apply. If there are additional co-attorneys please complete the Attorney Name, Relationship, Address and Date details in the 'Additional Information' section (at the end of this form).

Are all the attorneys applying to register?   Yes ○   No ○

If no, I (We) have given notice to my (our) co-attorney(s) as follows:

Name	Relationship to Donor	Address

Date notice given:

D D   M M   Y Y Y Y

Name	Relationship to Donor	Address

Date notice given:

D D   M M   Y Y Y Y

Part Nine - Fees

Guidelines on remission postponement of fees can be obtained from the Court of Protection.

Have you enclosed a cheque for the registration fee for this application?   Yes ☑   No ○

Do you wish to apply for postponement or remission of the fee?   Yes ○   No ☑

If yes, please give details below:

Part Ten - Declaration

Note: The application should be signed by all attorneys who are making the application. This must not pre-date the date(s) when the notices were given.

I (We) certify that the above information is correct and that to the best of my (our) knowledge and belief I (We) have complied with the provisions of the Enduring Powers of Attorney Act 1985 and all of the Rules and Regulations.

Signed: *Gillian Ross*   Dated: 1 9 0 8 2 0 0 3
                                   D D M M Y Y Y Y

Signed: Dated:
                   D D M M Y Y Y Y

Signed: Dated:

Continued overleaf   D D M M Y Y Y Y

Application for registration (Form EP2) (continued)

Part Eleven - Correspondence Address

Please state the address to which the correspondence should be sent if this is different to the address of Attorney One. State the full name and present address. If applicable, include the Company Name in Address Line 1.

Mr ○   Mrs ○   Ms ○   Miss ○   Other ○

If Other, please specify here:

Last Name:

Forename 1:

Other Forenames:

Address 1:

Address 2:

Address 3:

Town/City:

County:

Postcode:

DX No. (solicitors only):

DX Exchange (solicitors only):

Attorney Date of Birth:

D D   M M   Y Y Y Y

Occupation:

Daytime Tel No.:

Email Address:

Part Twelve - Additional Information

Please write down any additional information to support this application in the space below. If necessary attach additional paper to the end of this form.

Form EP3

Court of Protection

Enduring Powers of Attorney Act 1985

In the matter of a power given by

If this application is being made prior to an application for registration the original enduring power of attorney should accompany this application.

.... DAVID PETER ROSS .... (a donor)

to .... GILLIAN ROSS .... (attorney)

and .... (attorney)

General form of application

I ... GILLIAN ROSS ....

of .5 MAPLE TERRACE, LONDON, SW10 2PZ ....

and I ....

of ....

Note. Give details of the order or directions that you are seeking.

Apply for an order or directions that ... I BE PERMANENTLY
APPOINTED TO HANDLE THE AFFAIRS OF DAVID
PETER ROSS AS HIS ATTORNEY UNDER AN ENDURING
POWER OF ATTORNEY DATED 10TH APRIL 2003

State under which sub-section of the Enduring Powers of Attorney Act 1985 or which rule of the Court of Protection (Enduring Powers of Attorney) Rules 1994 this application is made.

and for any other directions which are necessary as a result of my/our application.

Note. Give details of the grounds on which you are seeking the order or directions.

The grounds on which I/we make this applications are:

THAT THE DONOR HAS BECOME MENTALLY INCAPABLE
TO HANDLE HIS OWN AFFAIRS.

Evidence in support should accompany this application.

Signed *Gillian Ross* .... Dated 10/06/03

Note. The application should be signed by all the applicants or their solicitors.

Signed .... Dated ....

Address where notices should be sent ....

.5 MAPLE TERRACE, LONDON, SW10 2PZ ....

GENERAL POWER OF ATTORNEY

(Pursuant to the Powers of Attorney Act 1971, section 10)

THIS GENERAL POWER OF ATTORNEY is made

this __3RD__ day of _____DECEMBER_____ year 2003

BY   MATTHEW JAMES ROSS

   OF   52 ARTILLERY STREET LONDON E13 7SL

I APPOINT   JONATHAN EDWARD SPENCER OF 22 MAPLE TERRACE LONDON SW10 7XA

AND SARAH JANE SPENCER OF 22 MAPLE TERRACE LONDON SW10 7XA

[jointly][jointly and severally] to be my attorney(s) in accordance with section 10 of the Powers of Attorney Act 1971.

IN WITNESS whereof I have hereunto set my hand the day and year first above written.

SIGNED as a Deed and Delivered by the said

M J Ross   MATTHEW JAMES ROSS

in the presence of:

Signature   *Andrew Kennington*

Full name   ANDREW PETER KENNINGTON

Address   216 COLE STREET

                 LONDON SE98 2XD

Occupation   WEBSITE DESIGNER

LIVING WILL

PERSONAL DETAILS

Name __DAVID PETER ROSS__

Address __5 MAPLE TERRACE, LONDON, SW10 2PZ__

Date of Birth __20TH JUNE 1937__

Doctor's details __DR JOHN FINLAY 020 7111 2233__

National Health Number __01234 56789__

I, _____DAVID PETER ROSS_____, am of sound mind and make this Advance Directive now on my future medical care to my family, my doctors, other medical personnel and any-one else to whom it is relevant, for a time when, for reasons of physical or mental incapacity, I am unable to make my views known.

INSTRUCTIONS

Medical treatment I DO NOT want

I REFUSE medical procedures to prolong my life or keep me alive by artificial means if:-

(1) ~~I have a severe physical illness from which, in the opinion of _____ independent medical practitioners, it is unlikely that I will ever recover;~~ ☐

or

(2) I have a severe mental illness which, in the opinion of __TWO__ independent medical practitioners, has no likelihood of improvement and in addition I have a severe physical illness from which, in the opinion of __TWO__ independent medical practitioners, it is unlikely that I will ever recover; ☑

or

(3) I am permanently unconscious and have been so for a period of at least __6__ months and in the opinion of two independent medical practitioners there is no likelihood that I will ever recover. ☑

Medical treatment I DO want

I DO wish to receive any medical treatment which will alleviate pain or distressing symptoms or will make me more comfortable. I accept that this may have the effect of shortening my life. ☑

~~[If I am suffering from any of the conditions above and I am pregnant, I wish to RECEIVE medical procedures which will prolong my life or keep me alive by artificial means only until such time as my child has been safely delivered.]~~

HEALTH CARE PROXY

I wish to appoint _____ MRS GILLIAN ROSS _____ of _____
5 MAPLE TERRACE, LONDON, SW10 2PZ _____ as my Health Care Proxy. S/he should be involved in any decisions about my health care options if I am physically or mentally unable to make my views known. I wish to make it clear that s/he is fully aware of my wishes and I request that his/her decisions be respected.

ADDITIONAL DIRECTIONS ON FUTURE HEALTH CARE

NONE

SIGNATURES

Signature *David P Ross* _____ Date 10TH APRIL 2003

Witness' Signature *Thomas White* _____ Date 10TH APRIL 2003

I confirm that my views are still as stated above.

	Date	Signature	Witness's Signature
1)			
2)			
3)			
4)			

SCOTLAND

CONTINUING POWER OF ATTORNEY

I, DAVID PETER ROSS

residing at 5 MAPLE TERRACE, GLASGOW, G10 2PZ

CONSIDERING that I find it convenient to appoint a proper person to manage my affairs whether or not I may hereafter be incapacitated THEREFORE I HEREBY APPOINT

MRS GILLIAN ROSS OF 5 MAPLE TERRACE, GLASGOW, G10 2PZ

* delete as appropriate

*[OR EITHER OF THEM acting jointly or severally] / [acting together and the survivor of them], to be my Factor and Commissioner and Attorney (hereinafter referred to as 'my Attorney') with full power for me and in my name or in his name as my Attorney both while I have capacity to grant this power and while I may cease to have capacity to grant this power, as a Continuing Power of Attorney to do everything, subject to all and any limitations and/or restrictions specified at the end of this Continuing Power of Attorney, which I could or can myself do regarding my estate of whatever nature and wherever situated both capital and income and whether now belonging or which may hereafter belong to me all which and each and every part thereof are hereinafter referred to and included under the expression 'my estate';

AND WITHOUT PREJUDICE to the foregoing generality I confer on my Attorney the following powers all to be exercised as he in his sole discretion may think fit namely:

(First) to give receipts and discharges and to pursue claims, debts and monies due to me and to sue for same in any appropriate Court of Law and to receive transference and payment of my estate;

(Second) to sign and endorse warrants and cheques; to operate Bank Accounts in my name; and to procure the issue of Warrants and cheques in name of my Attorney;

(Third) to carry through all income tax matters and business including the making of all claims for repayment of tax;

(Fourth) to purchase and/or sell by public auction or private contract or to let or to take on let property, goods, equipment or services and to enter into an agreement with a Building Society, Bank or other party relative to a loan or the provision of mortgage facilities;

(Fifth) to sign, seal, execute and deliver all conveyances, transfers, discharges and other writings and documents and to attend meetings and vote as my proxy;

(Sixth) to take up and pay for additional or bonus shares which may be offered by any Company in respect of any securities or investments in such Company held by me to change my investments or to make investments on similar or other lines and without restriction to the class of trust investments and to sign all relevant transfers, letters of allotment, forms of acceptance and/or renunciation and other documents; and

(Seventh) to claim and receive on my behalf all pensions, benefits and allowances to which I may be entitled.

AND I PROVIDE AND DECLARE THAT

(1) the powers hereby conferred on my Attorney shall be exercisable by my Attorney both while I am able to exercise such powers and continuing thereafter during any period in which I may be incapacitated,

(2) the effect of this Continuing Power of Attorney has been personally explained to me before my subscription hereof by the Prescribed Person who has added his certificate hereto,

(3) my Attorney shall incur no responsibility on account or in respect of his actings, intromissions, management, realisation, retention, renewal or making of investments or on any account whatever, fraud only excepted,

(4) these presents shall subsist till recalled in writing and the same shall be available and effectual to my Attorney and to third parties till they have actual notice of such recall and further I declare that these presents shall continuously subsist in force and operation notwithstanding that I may concurrently myself act in matters which may fall within the scope of these presents; Provided that my Attorney shall be bound as by acceptance hereof he binds himself to hold count and reckoning with me and my representatives for his intromissions in virtue of these presents, and

(5) in this document where the context so requires references to the masculine gender shall be deemed to include references to the feminine gender and references to the singular shall be deemed to include references to the plural.

Limitations and/or restrictions on powers granted by the foregoing Continuing Power of Attorney:

NONE

SIGNED by me the said _David P. Ross_

at __5 MAPLE TERRACE, GLASGOW, G10 2PZ__

on the __TENTH__ day of __APRIL__ Two Thousand and __THREE__

before this witness:

Witness : _Thomas Waite_

FULL NAME : THOMAS STEWART WAITE

Address : 36 AMBER ROAD, GLASGOW, G3 5HM

Occupation : PLUMBER

Note: This Continuing Power of Attorney when completed should be submitted along with the Certificate completed by a Prescribed Person attached and the form of application for registration attached to: The Office of the Public Guardian, Hadrian House, Callendar Business Park, Callendar Road, Falkirk, FK1 1XR, along with the appropriate fee (at present £35.00).

SCOTLAND CERTIFICATE FOR CPA

CERTIFICATE UNDER SECTION 15(3)(C) OF THE ADULTS WITH INCAPACITY (SCOTLAND) ACT 2000 TO
BE INCORPORATED IN A DOCUMENT GRANTING A CONTINUING POWER OF ATTORNEY
BY A SOLICITOR OR A PRACTISING MEMBER OF THE FACULTY OF ADVOCATES
OR A REGISTERED MEDICAL PRACTITIONER.

INSERT *NAMES AND* *DATE*	This Certificate is incorporated in the document subscribed by **DAVID PETER ROSS** ('the granter') on **10TH APRIL 2003** that confers a Continuing Power of Attorney on **MRS GILLIAN ROSS**
INSERT DATE	I certify that:- A. I interviewed the granter on **8TH APRIL 2003** immediately before he/she subscribed this Continuing Power of Attorney AND B. I am satisfied that, at the time this Continuing Power of Attorney was granted, the granter understood its nature and extent I have satisfied myself of this:
DELETE either [a] or [b] if not applicable. *Both MAY apply but one MUST apply*	[a] because of my own knowledge of the granter; [b] because I have consulted the following persons, who have knowledge of the granter on the matter:
INSERT names, designations, addresses *and relationships with granter, if any*	**I AM HIS DOCTOR** AND C. I have no reason to believe that the granter was acting under undue influence or that any other factor vitiates the granting of this continuing Power of Attorney.
INCLUDE full name and state whether address *given is business or personal*	Signed: ***Dr. Alan Henman*** Date: **15th APRIL 2003** Print Name: **DR ALAN PAUL HENMAN** Profession: **61 SADDLER STREET** Address: **EDINBURGH E4 7BY** NOTE: any person signing this certificate should not be the person to whom this Continuing Power of Attorney has been granted.

SCOTLAND

GENERAL POWER OF ATTORNEY

I,   MATTHEW JAMES ROSS

residing at   52 ARTILLERY STREET, GLASGOW,

G13 7SL

CONSIDERING that I find it convenient to appoint a proper person to manage my affairs while I have capacity to grant this General Power of Attorney THEREFORE I HEREBY APPOINT

JONATHAN EDWARD SPENCER OF 22 MAPLE TERRACE,

GLASGOW, G10 7XA

* delete as appropriate *~~[OR EITHER OF THEM acting jointly or severally]/[acting together and the survivor of them]~~ to be my Factor and Commissioner and Attorney (hereinafter referred to as 'my Attorney') with full power for me and in my name or in his name as my Attorney (without any need for registration with the Public Guardian) to do everything, subject to all and any limitations and/or restrictions specified at the end of this General Power of Attorney, which I could or can myself do regarding my estate of whatever nature and wherever situated both capital and income and whether now belonging or which may hereafter belong to me all which and each and every part thereof are hereinafter referred to and included under the expression 'my estate';

AND WITHOUT PREJUDICE to the foregoing generality I confer on my Attorney the following powers all to be exercised as he in his sole discretion may think fit namely:

(First) to give receipts and discharges and to pursue claims, debts and monies due to me and to sue for same in any appropriate Court of Law and to receive transference and payment of my estate;

(Second) to sign and endorse warrants and cheques to operate Bank Accounts in my name and to procure the issue of warrants and cheques in name of my Attorney;

(Third) to carry through all income tax matters including the making of all claims for repayment of tax;

(Fourth) to purchase and/or sell by public auction or private contract or to let or to take on let property, goods, equipment or services and to enter into an agreement with a Building Society, Bank or other party relative to a loan or the provision of mortgage facilities:

(Fifth) to sign, seal, execute and deliver all conveyances, transfers, discharges and other writings and documents and to attend meetings and vote as my proxy;

(Sixth) to take up and pay for additional or bonus shares which may be offered by any Company in respect of any securities or investments in such Company held by me to change my investments or to make investments on similar or other lines and without restriction to the class of trust investments and to sign all relevant transfers, letters of allotment, forms of acceptance and/or renunciation and other documents; and

(Seventh) to claim and receive on my behalf all pensions, benefits and allowances to which I may be entitled.

AND I PROVIDE AND DECLARE THAT

(1) the powers hereby conferred on my Attorney shall be exercisable by my Attorney only while I am able to exercise such powers,

(2) my Attorney shall incur no responsibility on account or in respect of his actings, intromissions, management, realisation, retention, renewal or making of investments or on any account whatever, fraud only excepted,

(3) these presents shall subsist till recalled in writing and the same shall be available and effectual to my Attorney and to third parties till they have actual notice of such recall and further I declare that these presents shall continuously subsist in force and operation notwithstanding that I may concurrently myself act in matters which may fall within the scope of these presents; Provided that my Attorney shall be bound as by acceptance hereof he binds himself to hold count and reckoning with me and my representatives for his intromissions in virtue of these presents, and

(4) in this document where the context so requires references to the masculine gender shall be deemed to include references to the feminine gender and references to the singular shall be deemed to include references to the plural.

Limitations and/or restrictions on powers granted by the foregoing General Power of Attorney:

NONE

SIGNED by me the said ___*M J Ross*___
at _52 ARTILLERY STREET, GLASGOW, G13 7SL_
on the _THIRD_ day of ___JULY___ Two Thousand and _THREE_
before this witness:

Witness : *Andrew Kennington*
FULL NAME : ANDREW PETER KENNINGTON
Address : 216 COLE STREET
GLASGOW G98 2XD
Occupation : WEBSITE DESIGNER

SCOTLAND

WELFARE POWER OF ATTORNEY

I,   CHARLOTTE HEATH

residing at   17 TOOLEY ROAD, EDINBURGH, EH4 9WX

CONSIDERING that I find it convenient to appoint a proper person to deal with and make determinations in regard to matters affecting my welfare when I may be incapacitated THEREFORE I HEREBY APPOINT

RICHARD HEATH

17 TOOLEY ROAD, EDINBURGH, EH4 9WX

* delete as appropriate

*[OR EITHER OF THEM acting jointly or severally]/[acting together and the survivor of them], to be my Factor and Commissioner and Attorney (hereinafter referred to as 'my Welfare Attorney') with full power for me and in my name or in his name as my Welfare Attorney to deal with subject to all and any limitations and/or restrictions specified at the end of this Welfare Power of Attorney and determine and give instructions on all matters relating to my welfare during all and any periods when I may be incapacitated;

AND I PROVIDE AND DECLARE THAT
(1) my Welfare Attorney shall before acting in terms hereof, register this Welfare Power of Attorney with the Public Guardian,
(2) the effect of this Welfare Power of Attorney has been personally explained to me before my subscription hereof by the Prescribed Person who has added his certificate hereto,
(3) my Welfare Attorney shall incur no responsibility or liability on account or in respect of his actings or determinations in the exercise of this Welfare Power of Attorney,
(4) my Welfare Attorney shall be entitled to act, if a Solicitor, on my behalf as my Solicitor, to employ Solicitors and others and generally to do all things and make determinations and give instructions in regard to my welfare that I might myself do or make but for my incapacity,
(5) these presents shall subsist till effectively recalled in writing and the same shall be available and effectual to my Welfare Attorney and to third parties till they have actual notice of such recall, and
(6) in this document where the context so requires references to the masculine gender shall be deemed to include references to the feminine gender and references to the singular shall be deemed to include references to the plural.

Limitations and/or restrictions on powers granted by the foregoing Welfare Power of Attorney:

NONE

SIGNED by me the said   *Charlotte Heath*

at   17 TOOLEY ROAD, EDINBURGH, EH4 9WX

on the __THIRD__ day of __JULY__ Two Thousand and __THREE__

before this witness:

Witness :   *Virginia Coles*

FULL NAME :   VIRGINIA CLARE COLES

Address :   42 GATWICK ROAD

EDINBURGH EH3 2CA

Occupation :   ARTIST

Note: This Welfare Power of Attorney when completed should be submitted along with the Certificate completed by a Prescribed Person attached and the form of application for registration attached to: The Office of the Public Guardian, Hadrian House, Callendar Business Park, Callendar Road, Falkirk, FK1 1XR, along with the appropriate fee (at present £35.00).

© 2003 Law Pack Publishing Limited

SCOTLAND CERTIFICATE FOR WPA

CERTIFICATE UNDER SECTION 16(3)(C) OF THE ADULTS WITH INCAPACITY (SCOTLAND) ACT 2000 TO BE INCORPORATED IN A DOCUMENT GRANTING A WELFARE POWER OF ATTORNEY BY A SOLICITOR OR A PRACTISING MEMBER OF THE FACULTY OF ADVOCATES OR A REGISTERED MEDICAL PRACTITIONER.

INSERT NAMES AND DATE	This Certificate is incorporated in the document subscribed by **CHARLOTTE HEATH** ('the granter') on **3RD JULY 2003** that confers a Welfare Power of Attorney on **RICHARD HEATH**
INSERT DATE	I certify that:- A. I interviewed the granter on **1ST JULY 2003** immediately before he/she subscribed this Welfare Power of Attorney AND B. I am satisfied that, at the time this Welfare Power of Attorney was granted, the granter understood its nature and extent I have satisfied myself of this:
DELETE either [a] or [b] if not applicable. Both MAY apply but one MUST apply	[a] because of my own knowledge of the granter; ~~[b] because I have consulted the following persons, who have knowledge of the granter on the matter:~~
INSERT names, designations, addresses and relationships with granter, if any	**I AM THE FAMILY SOLICITOR OF THE GRANTER** AND C. I have no reason to believe that the granter was acting under undue influence or that any other factor vitiates the granting of this Welfare Power of Attorney.
INCLUDE full name and state whether address given is business or personal	Signed: *Stewart Collins* Date: **12TH JULY 2003** Print Name: **STEWART ALAN COLLINS** Profession: **SOLICITOR** Address: **91 KINGSWAY AVENUE** **EDINGBURGH EH42 7UY** NOTE: any person signing this certificate should not be the person to whom this Welfare Power of Attorney has been granted.

ADULTS WITH INCAPACITY (SCOTLAND) ACT 2000

APPLICATION FOR REGISTRATION OF A CONTINUING POWER OF ATTORNEY OR WELFARE POWER OF ATTORNEY

Section 1 - Details of Granter

Title Mr/Mrs/Miss/Other MR

Surname ROSS

Forename(s) DAVID

Other Names PETER

Date of Birth 20/06/30

Address

House Name

House Number 5

Street Name MAPLE TERRACE

Town GLASGOW G10 2FZ

Post Code G10 2PZ

Telephone Number including area code 01234 56789

Email Address DAVROSS@LAWPACK.CO.UK

Ethnic Origin of Granter   (Please tick as appropriate)

African	☐	Oriental	☐
Afro-Caribbean	☐	White	☑
Asian	☐		

Other (please specify)

ADULTS WITH INCAPACITY (SCOTLAND) ACT 2000

Section 2 - Nature of Power

(Please tick either or both)

Continuing ☑   Welfare ☐

Section 3 - Details of: The Attorney   Joint Attorney

	The Attorney	Joint Attorney
Title Mr/Mrs/Miss/Other	MRS	
Surname	ROSS	
Forename(s)	GILLIAN	
Other Names		

Address

	The Attorney	Joint Attorney
Company Name		
House Name		
House Number	5	
Street Name	MAPLE TERRACE	
Town	GLASGOW	
Post Code	G10 2PZ	
Telephone Number including area code	01234 56789	
Email Address	GILROSS@LAWPACK.CO.UK	

Type of Appointment   (Please tick as appropriate)

Continuing ☑ Welfare ☐   Continuing ☐ Welfare ☐

ADULTS WITH INCAPACITY (SCOTLAND) ACT 2000

Relationship to Granter   (Please tick as appropriate)

Relative ☑   Professional ☐   Friend/Other ☐

If relative please give details

WIFE

Confirmation that Attorney is willing to act

	I confirm that I am willing to act as Attorney	I confirm that I am willing to act as Joint Attorney
Signed	*Gillian Ross*	
Date	20/04/03	

ADULTS WITH INCAPACITY (SCOTLAND) ACT 2000

Section 4 - **Details of the Sender**

When the power of attorney is registered, the Certif cate of Registration will be issued to the sender. Please give details of the sender.

Title Mr/Mrs/Miss/Other   MRS

Surname   ROSS

Forename(s)   GILLIAN

Name of Company

Address

House Number   5

Street Name   MAPLE TERRACE

Town   GLASGOW

Post Code   G10 2PZ

Telephone Number
including area code   01234 56789

Email Address   GILROSS@LAWPACK.CO.UK

If a substitute attorney has been nominated please complete section 5

ADULTS WITH INCAPACITY (SCOTLAND) ACT 2000

Section 5 - Details of any Substitute Attorneys appointed

	First Substitute Attorney	Second Substitute Attorney
Title Mr/Mrs/Miss/Other	MR	
Surname	WAITE	
Forename(s)	THOMAS	
Other Names	BENJAMIN	

Address

House Name		
House Number	36	
Street Name	AMBER ROAD	
Town	GLASGOW	
Post Code	G3 5HM	

Telephone Number including area code	01567 89012	
Email Address	TWAITE@LAWPACK.CO.UK	

Type of Appointment   (Please tick as appropriate)

Continuing ☐   Welfare ☑   Continuing ☐   Welfare ☐

Relationship to Granter   (Please tick as appropriate)

Relative ☐   Professional ☐   Friend/Other ☑

If relative please give details

If more Attorneys have been nominated and appointed please continue on a separate sheet of paper.

ADULTS WITH INCAPACITY (SCOTLAND) ACT 2000

Section 6 - Details of persons to whom a copy of the power of attorney should be sent

If a requirement is contained within the Power of Attorney that when registered a copy is sent to up to two specified persons please provide the following detail

	First Specified Person	Second Specified Person
Title Mr/Mrs/Miss/Other	MRS	MR
Surname	ROSS	WAITE
Forename(s)	GILLIAN	THOMAS
Other Names		BENJAMIN
Address		
House Name		
House Number	5	36
Street Name	MAPLE TERRACE	AMBER ROAD
Town	GLASGOW	GLASGOW
Post Code	G10 2PZ	G3 5HM
Telephone Number including area code	01234 56789	01567 89012
Email Address	GILROSS@LAWPACK.CO.UK	TWAITE@LAWPACK.CO.UK

Probate forms

Form PA1 - Probate application

Probate application form

Please read the booklet HOW TO OBTAIN PROBATE

USE CAPITAL LETTERS

At which Probate Registry or local office do you want to be interviewed? (See pages 6-12 of the booklet)	**SECTION 1** BRISTOL PROBATE REGISTRY	This Column is for official use

	SECTION 2 **Details of the deceased**	
1 Surname	SCOTT	
2 Fornames	EDWARD JOHN	True Name
3 Are any assets held in another name?		
If YES, what are the assets?	Answer YES or NO NO	
and in what name(s) are they held?		Alias
		Address
4 Address of the deceased	16 JAMES COURT	
	BATH BA7 4NH	F/O
5 Occupation of deceased at time of death. State RETIRED or OF NO OCCUPATION if applicable	SALES MANAGER	D/C district & no
6 Date of death	27TH JULY 2003 Age 56	
7 Date of birth	2ND FEBRUARY 1947	L.S.A. D.B.F.

8   TICK the **legal** marital status of the deceased, and give dates where appropriate

Bachelor	☐	
Spinster	☐	
Widowed	☐	
Married	☑	date 4/5/91
Divorced	☐	date _____
Legally separated	☐	date _____

FORM PA1 (3/95)

Reproduced by Law Pack Publishing with the permission of the Controller of HMSO

SECTION 3   **The Will**

		This Column is for official use

1 Did the deceased leave a will?
PLEASE NOTE that a will may not necessarily be a formal document

Answer YES or NO   YES

Date of will/codicil

2 Is there anyone under 18 years old who receives a gift in the will?

Answer YES or NO   NO

3 Are there any executors named in the will?

Answer YES or NO   YES

4 Give the name(s) of those executors who are not applying and reason A, B, C or D

Reason A,B,C,D

NOT APPLICABLE

A - died before the deceased
B - died after the deceased
C - does not wish to apply
D - does not wish to apply now but may later

SECTION 4   **Relatives of the deceased**

	NUMBER *If none cross through each box*	
	over 18	under 18
Sons or daughters who survived the deceased	2	
Sons or daughters who did not survive the deceased	0	
Their children who survived the deceased		
Parents who survived the deceased	1	
Brothers or sisters who survived the deceased	1	
Brothers or sisters who did not survive the deceased	0	
Their children who survived the deceased		
Grandparents who survived the deceased	0	——

1 Give the **number** of relatives, over 18 and under 18 years old in each category
If none cross through each box
PLEASE NOTE survived means they were alive when the deceased died

2 Was the deceased adopted?   Answer YES or NO   NO

3 Has any relative of the deceased been adopted?   Answer YES or NO   NO

If YES give their name(s) and relationship(s) to the deceased:

Answer questions 4, 5 and 6 only if the deceased died before 4th April 1988 or left a will or codicil dated before that date.

4 Was the deceased illegitimate?   Answer YES or NO

5 Did the deceased leave any illegitimate sons or daughters?   Answer YES or NO

6 Did the deceased have any illegitimate sons or daughters who died leaving children of their own?   Answer YES or NO

SECTION 5   Details of applicant

This Column is for official use

PLEASE NOTE that the grant will normally be sent to the first applicant

Tick correct box

1 Title   Mr ☐   Mrs ☐   Miss ✔

2 Forenames   MELANIE

3 Surname   SCOTT

I.T.W.C.

4 Address   17 ARUNDEL WAY

BRISTOL

Postcode   BS8 3JQ

5 Occupation/marital status   ACCOUNTANT / SINGLE

6 Tel. No.   at home 0117 123456 at work 0117 654321

7 Are you related to the deceased?   Answer YES or NO   YES

8 *If YES* what is your relationship in law?   DAUGHTER

9 Name and address of any surviving husband or wife of the deceased, unless stated above   JULIA ANNE SCOTT

If there are any other applicants give their details as shown above

Details of other applicants who wish to be named in the grant of administration and attend the interview

ROSEMARY JANE RAYNER

98 CHURCHILL ROAD

SWINDON SN9 4SZ

OCCUPATION: TEACHER

MARITAL STATUS: MARRIED

TELEPHONE NO.(HOME): 01793 355688

TELEPHONE NO.(WORK): 01793 111666

When you return this form you MUST also send:

- **The original death certificate**
- **The original will (if there is one)**
- **The account of the estate (IHT200 or IHT 205)**

Now please refer to the booklet for the address to which you should send your application

This page is for official use

Will not sent
Death certificate not sent
Domicile
Minority/Life interest
Title of grant

Faulty clause/no clause
Date
Signature
Alterations
Incorporation
Gift to witness/spouse of witness
Gift to issue S.33
Power reserved/renunciation/attorney

Clearing

Domiciled in England and Wales

Title

PR to other
execut
+ F.N.

Limitation

For the use and benefit of the said ....
and until further representation be granted

Affidavit of:-

MI or LI

Gross N.E.   £_____
Net N.E.   £_____

FOR OATH AND FEES

Gross   £_____
Less debts   £_____
Net
Less CSG   £_____
For fees   £_____
Fees—Court   £_____
Dept   £_____
Total
Fees for
copies   £_____
Total   _____

GROSS FOR REVENUE PURPOSES (Net estate for
tax purposes)

Gross non-option   £
Gross option   £
Gross joint   £
Nominated   £
Foreign   £
Trusts etc   £
Gifts   £_____
Gross Total   £

FOR IHT 202

Net joint realty   £
Net joint personalty   £
Nominated   £_____
Total 6   _____

For probate purposes
Total 7   £_____

(Real and personal)
Less debts   £_____
Total 8   _____

(net estate for
probate purposes)
Total 6   £
plus Total 8   £_____
Total 9   £_____

FOR IHT 200

1A Gross non-option   £_____
Less debts   £_____
Net   £_____

1B Gross option   £_____
Less debts   £_____
Net   £_____

2A Non-option—
Joint personalty   £
Nominated   £
Foreign   £_____
Total
Less debts   £_____
Net   _____

2B Option—
Joint realty   £_____
Foreign   £_____
Total
Less debts   £_____
Net   _____

3 Trusts etc Total   £_____
Total net estate for Tax £

Revenue
Capital Taxes Office

Short Form for
Personal Applicants

Name of the person who has died

MICHAEL STEPHEN BROWN

Date when the person died*

15TH JUNE 2003

Inheritance Tax

*Use this form only if the person died after 5 April 1998

Introduction

Do you need to fill in a full Inland Revenue Account before you can get a grant of probate?

Probate fees and any Inheritance Tax and interest due have to be worked out and paid before you can get a grant of probate or letters of administration.

Estates which meet certain conditions are called "excepted estates". If the estate of the person who has died is an excepted estate, you do not need to fill in a full Inheritance Tax Account. You can fill in this form instead.

Before you start to fill in this form, read the introduction in the booklet IHT 206. This will help you to decide whether you should fill in this form or a full Inheritance Tax Account on form IHT 200.

Question 1
Where was the domicile of the person who has died? (Please tick one box only.)

England and Wales ☑   Scotland ☐

Northern Ireland ☐   Other ☐

If you ticked "other", do not fill in any more of this form. Instead you will need to fill in a full Inland Revenue Account on form IHT200. You can get one by telephoning Capital Taxes Office on 0845 2341020. This is an answer phone service.

If you did not tick "other" please answer the questions on page 2. If you answer 'No' to all of them, look at the booklet IHT 206 again to help you to fill in pages 3 and 4. **If you find that you need more space, use a separate sheet of paper and show clearly which part of the form the sheet refers to.** When you have filled in the whole form and signed it, return it to the Probate Registry with form PA1.

Do you need help?

If you have any questions about **Inheritance Tax** or how to fill in this form, please write to:-

Inland Revenue, Capital Taxes Office, Ferrers House, PO Box 38, Castle Meadow Road, Nottingham, NG2 1BB

or telephone 0115 974 2400.(please do not use this number just to order form IHT200).

If you have any questions about **Probate** matters, please contact your local District Probate Registry.

Questions			Please tick	
			Yes	**No**
2.	**Gifts**			
	Did the person who has died within 7 years of the date they died,			
	a	make any gifts or set up a trust? (but see note on page 2 of IHT206)	☐	☑
	b	make any payment(s) of more than £10,000 in total for the maintenance of a relative?	☐	☑
	c	pay any premiums on a life insurance policy under which the benefit is not payable to the personal representative or to the husband or wife of the person who has died?	☐	☑
3.	Did the person who has died make a **gift with reservation** at any time?		☐	☑
4.	**Assets held in trust**			
	Was the person who has died receiving a benefit under a trust			
	•	at the time when they died	☐	☑
	•	at any time within 7 years before they died?	☐	☑
5.	**Foreign assets**			
	Did the person who has died own or benefit from any assets outside the United Kingdom whose value is more than £50,000?		☐	☑

If you have answered 'Yes' to any of these questions, do not fill in pages 3 and 4 of this form..
Instead you will need to fill in a full Inland Revenue Account on form IHT200.

You can get one from Capital Taxes Office by telephoning our Orderline on 0845 2341020. This is an answer phone service. We will aim to send forms out to you by the end of the next working day.

Return of the whole estate

Assets in the United Kingdom except for joint assets passing automatically to the surviving joint owner.

Value in £s

1. Cash other than at bank ... ... NIL

2. Money in bank accounts 2,592

3. Money in building societies, co-operative or friendly societies or savings banks including interest to the date of death 10,324

4. Household and personal goods, *for example, furniture, jewellery, car, stamp collections etc* 15,500

5. Savings Certificates and other National Savings investments ... ... NIL

6. Stocks and shares quoted on the Stock Exchange ... ... NIL

7. Stocks and shares not quoted on the Stock Exchange ... ... NIL

8. Insurance policies including bonuses on 'with profits' policies and mortgage protection policies ... ... See..Schedule..1 15,250

9. Amounts which employers owe - including arrears of salary and pension payable to the estate ...State..retirement..pension 53

10. Partnership and business interests ... ... NIL

11. Freehold and leasehold property **in the sole name of the person who has died.** (Address(es)) ... ... NIL

12. Assets held as tenants in common ... ... NIL

13. Any other assets not included above, for example, income tax repayment, debt or other amount owing to the person who has died ...

Total £ 43,719 **A**

14. Assets outside the United Kingdom (Value in sterling) ... ... NIL

15. Nominated assets ... ... NIL

16. **Joint assets passing automatically to the surviving joint owner**

Details of joint assets ... ... SEE SCHEDULE 2 ... .

Value of whole of joint assets £ ...62,642... ... ...
Share of person who has died (eg half) half... Value of that share 31,321

Total gross estate (A + 14 + 15 + 16) = £ 75,040 **B**

17. **Gifts of cash, or stocks and shares quoted on the Stock Exchange** ... ...

Total for excepted estate (B + 17) = £ 75,040 **C***

* see the box on the back page of this form

3

18. Debts

Bills owing in the United Kingdom

Funeral expenses ... ...   £   975

Debts owed by the person who has died ... ..   £   92

Mortgage on a property in the name
of the person who has died ... ...   £   NIL

Total debts owing in the UK   £ | 1,067 | **D**

Debts owing to persons outside the UK ... ...   £   NIL   **P**

Debts secured on or payable out of joint assets ...   £   NIL   **Q**

Total debts (D+P+Q) =   £ | 1,067 | **E**

Net figure for Inheritance Tax (C minus E) ... ...   £ | 73,973 | **F**

Signature(s)   *Frances Brown*   *Richard Steward*

Date   1ST SEPTEMBER 2003   3RD SEPTEMBER 2003

* If the figure at C is less than £240,000 , you do not have to fill in a full Account on form IHT200. **However, the Capital Taxes Office has the right to call for an account within 35 days of the grant. It calls for an account in a small number of cases each year.** The Probate Registry will return this form to you when they issue the grant of probate. Please keep this form safe so that if you do receive a request for a full account from the Capital Taxes Office, you can send them a copy.

Unless they make such a request within 35 days of the date of the grant, you have automatic clearance from Inheritance Tax as long as you have made a full disclosure of all relevant facts.

Summary

Gross estate in United Kingdom passing under Will/intestacy   £ | | **A**

Debts in United Kingdom owed by deceased alone   £ | | **D**

Net estate in United Kingdom (A minus D)   £ | | **G**

4

MICHAEL STEPHEN BROWN (date of death 15th June 2003)

Schedule 1 to Form IHT 205

Insurance policies

		£	£
1.	Norwich Union whole life policy	12,300	
2.	Sun Life whole life policy	2,950	
TOTAL:			15,250

Schedule 2 to Form IHT 205

Joint assets passing automatically by survivorship

		£	£
1.	Freehold house: 17 Peter Street Ipswich, IP15 2JH owned jointly with wife, Frances Jane Brown	60,000	
2.	Lloyds Bank current account owned jointly with wife, Frances Jane Brown	2,642	
TOTAL:			62,642
deceased's half share			31,321

5

**Assent of whole
of registered title(s)**

HM Land Registry

AS1

(if you need more room than is provided for in a panel, use continuation sheet CS and staple to this form)

1. Title Number(s) of the Property *(leave blank if not yet registered)*

XYZ 123456

2. Property

16 JAMES COURT, BATH BA7 4NH

If this assent is made under section 37 of the Land Registration Act 1925 following a not-yet-registered dealing with part only of the land in a title, or is made under rule 72 of the Land Registration Rules 1925, include a reference to the last preceding document of title containing a description of the property.

3. Date   30/9/03

4. Name of deceased proprietor *(give full names)*

EDWARD JOHN SCOTT

5. Personal Representative of deceased proprietor *(give full names and Company's Registered Number if any)*

MELANIE SCOTT of 17 Arundel Way, Bristol BS8 3JQ and
ROSEMARY JANE RAYNER of 98 Churchill Road, Swindon SN9 4SZ

6. Recipient **for entry on the register** *(Give full names and Company's Registered Number if any: for Scottish Co. Reg. Nos. use an SC prefix. For foreign companies give territory in which incorporated.)*

MELANIE SCOTT

Unless otherwise arranged with Land Registry headquarters, a certified copy of the transferee's constitution (in English or Welsh) will be required if it is a body corporate but is not a company registered in England and Wales or Scotland under the Companies Acts.

7. Recipient's intended **address(es) for service in the U.K.** *(including postcode)* for entry on the register

17 ARUNDEL WAY, BRISTOL BS8 3JQ

8. The Personal Representative assents to the vesting of the property in the Recipient.

9. The Personal Representative assents with *(place "X" in the box which applies and add any modifications)*

☐ full title guarantee   ☑ limited title guarantee

10. Declaration of trust *Where there is more than one recipient, place "X" in the appropriate box.*

☐ The recipients are to hold the property on trust for themselves as joint tenants.

☐ The recipients are to hold the property on trust for themselves as tenants in common in equal shares.

☐ The recipients are to hold the property *(complete as necessary)*

Reproduced by Law Pack Publishing with the permission of the Controller of HMSO   Crown copyright (ref: LR/SC.3)

11. Additional Provision(s) *Insert here any required or permitted statement, certificate or application and any agreed covenants, declarations, etc.*

12. *The Personal Representatives and all other necessary parties should sign this assent in the presence of witnesses or execute it as a deed using the space below. Forms of execution are given in Schedule 3 to the Land Registration Rules 1925. If the assent contains recipients' covenants or declarations or contains an application by them (e.g. for a restriction), it must also be executed by the Recipients.*

Melanie Scott

Signed as a deed by (enter full name of individual) in the presence of:

Sign here
Melanie Scott

Signature of witness .... *John Smith*
Name (in **BLOCK CAPITALS**) ...... JOHN SMITH
Address .... 25 GLOUCESTER GARDENS, BRISTOL BS2 4PP

Rosemary Jane
Rayner

Signed as a deed by (enter full name of individual) in the presence of:

Sign here
R Rayner

Signature of witness .... *Lesley Jones*
Name (in **BLOCK CAPITALS**) ...... LESLEY JONES
Address .... 117 FENNER WAY, BRISTOL BS9 3XG

(Introduced 4/98)

Confirmation

Your name and address

MISS MELANIE SCOTT
17 ARUNDEL WAY
GLASGOW
G4 SJQ

Your reference

IR CT reference

About the person who has died

Surname

SCOTT

Title

MR

Forenames

EDWARD JOHN

Occupation

SALES MANAGER

Date of birth

02/02/1947

Date of death

27/07/2003

Place of death

GLASGOW

Address

16 JAMES COURT
GLASGOW
G4 7UB

Testate/~~Intestate~~
(delete as appropriate)

Total estate for
Confirmation

£ 165,000.00

Executors

Full name(s) and address(es). If nominate, list in order shown in the will, etc.

MISS MELANIE SCOTT
17 ARUNDEL WAY   GLASGOW   G4 3LQ

MRS ROSEMARY JANE RAYNER
98 CHURCHILL ROAD   SWINDON   SN9 4SZ

20

Recorded in the Court Books of the

along with relative Deeds.

1

113415082000DTP

Form C1 Account - Application for Confirmation (continued)

Declaration by

MISS MELANIE SCOTT
17 ARUNDEL WAY
GLASGOW
G4 3JQ

1. who declares that the deceased (full name)

EDWARD JOHN SCOTT

died on the date and at the place shown on page 1

domiciled in

THE SHERIFFDOM OF GLASGOW AND STRATHKELVIN AT GLASGOW IN SCOTLAND

2. That I am

THE DAUGHTER AND EXECUTOR-NOMINATE OF THE SAID DECEASED ALONG WITH ROSEMARY JANE RAYNER OF 98 CHURCHILL ROAD, SWINDON CONFORM TO WILL BY THE SAID DECEASED DATED 10TH JUNE 1990 HEREWITH PRODUCED AND DOCQUETTED AS RELATIVE HERETO.

3. That I/ have entered or am/are about to enter, upon possession and management of the deceased's estate as Execut OR foresaid along with the said

MRS ROSEMARY JANE RAYNER

4. That I do not know of any testamentary settlement or writing relating to the disposal of the deceased's estate or any part of the deceased's estate other than that mentioned in paragraph 2.

5. That the Inventory (on pages 3 -) is a full and complete Inventory of the

- heritable estate in Scotland belonging to the deceased or the destination of which (s)he had the power to and did evacuate,
- moveable estate of the deceased in Scotland,
- real and personal estate of the deceased in England and Wales and in Northern Ireland,
- estate of the deceased situated elsewhere

including property, other than settled property over which (s)he had and exercised an absolute power of disposal.

6. That confirmation of the estate in Scotland, England and Wales and Northern Ireland amounting in value to £ 165,000.00 is required

All of which is true to the best of my knowledge and belief

Signature   Date

Warning to Executors

You may be liable to penalties or prosecution if you fail to make full enquiries and to include all property on which Inheritance Tax is payable.

2

Inventory

Inventory of

- the heritable estate in Scotland belonging to the deceased or the destination of which (s)he had power to and did evacuate,

- the moveable estate of the deceased in Scotland

- the real and personal estate of the deceased in England, Wales and Northern Ireland

- the estate of the deceased situated elsewhere

Include property, other than settled property, over which the deceased had and exercised an absolute power of disposal.

List the estate under these headings and in this order

Estate in Scotland (heritable property first)
Estate in England and Wales
Estate in Northern Ireland
Summary for confirmation
Estate elsewhere (say in which country)

Item No	Description	Price of shares	£
	ESTATE IN SCOTLAND		
	I. HERITABLE		
1.	DWELLINGHOUSE FORMING 16 JAMES COURT GLASGOW REGISTERED IN THE LAND REGISTER OF SCOTLAND UNDER TITLE NUMBER GLA14789 - ESTIMATED		£ 50,000.00
	II. MOVEABLE		
2.	THE ROYAL BANK OF SCOTLAND ACCOUNT 123456		£ 10,000.00
			£ 60,000.00
			==========
	ESTATE IN ENGLAND AND WALES		
3.	MARKS AND SPENCER PLC 20,000 ORDINARY SHARES	@ 3.40	£ 68,000.00
4.	PRUDENTIAL ASSURANCE POLICY NUMBER 144556		£ 37,000.00
			£105,000.00
			==========
		Carried forward	

3

Summary of amounts to be paid on this form

Tax and interest being paid now which may not be paid by instalments *(J1 1 on IHT200)*

NIL

Tax and interest being paid now which may be paid by instalments *(J18 on IHT200)*

NIL

Tax and interest being paid now on this form *(J19 on IHT200)*

NIL

For IR CT use only

IR CT Cashiers

Received this day the sum of

£

for Inheritance Tax and interest thereon

for Commissioners of Inland Revenue

The st amp and receipt are provisional.
The Inventory will be examined after it has been recorded and the amount of tax adjusted if necessary.

Additional information required for Commissary purposes

Joint property

W as the deceased a "joint owner" of any property Heritable or Moveable passing by survivorship? If so, identify the property , st ate the share and appropriate reason below.

No ✓ Yes

Value of share

Descendants surviving the deceased

State the number of any children or grandchildren who survived the deceased

Children	Grandchildren
2	4

Aggregate chargeable transfer

Enter the aggregate chargeable transfer *(box H15 on IHT200)*

£ 165,000.00

Enter the total liabilities at the death

£ 3,000.00

Is the estate an excepted estate?

No Yes ✓

Is the estate a small estate?

No ✓ Yes

Your telephone number

0141 123456

Inventory continued

Item No	Description	Price of shares	£
		~~brought forward~~	
	ESTATE IN NORTHERN IRELAND		==========
	SUMMARY FOR CONFIRMATION		

	ESTATE IN SCOTLAND
	    HERITABLE £50,000.00
	    MOVEABLE £10,000.00 £ 60,000.00		

	ESTATE IN ENGLAND AND WALES £105,000.00		
	ESTATE IN NORTHERN IRELAND £ 00.00		
	TOTAL FOR CONFIRMATION £165,000.00 ==========		
		~~carried forward~~	

C2

114429062000DTP

FORM OF DOCKET

I/We ___MISS MELANIE SCOTT___ of ___17 ARUNDEL WAY, GLASGOW, G4 3JQ___

and ___MRS ROSEMARY JANE RAYNER___ of ___98 CHURCHILL ROAD, SWINDON, SN9 4SZ___

being by virtue of the within ~~Confirmation~~/Certificate of Confirmation* the Executor(s) on the estate

of the deceased ___EDWARD JOHN SCOTT, SALES MANAGER LATE OF 16 JAMES COURT,___

___GLASGOW, G4 7UB___ so far as specified in the said ~~Confirmation~~/Certificate of Confirmation*

hereby NOMINATE ___ME THE SAID MISS MELANIE SCOTT___ as the person entitled:

(a) ~~in [part] satisfaction of his claim to prior rights, as a surviving spouse, on the death of the deceased;~~

(b) ~~in [part] satisfaction of his claim to legal rights on the death of the deceased;~~

(c) ~~in [part] satisfaction of his share of the said estate;~~

(d) in [part] implement of a ~~Trust Disposition and Settlement, [or~~ Will, ~~or as the case may be]~~ of the said deceased dated ___TENTH JUNE, NINETEEN HUNDRED AND NINETY___ ~~and registered in the Books of Council and Session~~

to the item of estate, ~~that is to say [*short desciption*] being number of~~ _____ ~~of the items of the estate~~, specified in the said ~~Confirmation~~/Certificate of Confirmation.* And I/We certify that this

Instrument falls within Category __E__ in the Schedule to the Stamp Duty (Exempt Instruments)

Regulations 1987.

SIGNED by *Melanie Scott* at ___17 ARUNDEL WAY, GLASGOW, G4 3JQ___
on the ___THIRTIETH___ day of ___MAY___ Two thousand and ___THREE___ before:

Witness ___John Smith___ Full name ___JOHN ROGER SMITH___
Address ___25 GLOUCESTER GARDENS, GLASGOW, G2 4PP___
Occupation ___BUILDER___

SIGNED by *Rosemary Rayner* at ___98 CHURCHILL ROAD, SWINDON, SN9 4SZ___
on the ___THIRTIETH___ day of ___MAY___ Two thousand and ___THREE___ before:

Witness ___Lesley Jones___ Full name ___LESLEY SARAH JONES___
Address ___117 FENNER WAY, SWINDON, SS9 3XG___
Occupation ___PERSONAL ASSISTANT___

* delete as necessary

Inland Revenue Account for Inheritance Tax

Fill in this account for the estate of a person who died on or after 18 March 1986.
You should read the related guidance note(s) before filling in any particular box(es).
The notes follow the same numbering as this form, so section headings are shown
by capital letters and the items in each section are on a dark background.

A **Probate Registry, Commissary Court or Sheriff Court District**

Name **A1** BRISTOL   Date of Grant

B **About the person who has died**

Title **B1** MR   Surname **B2** SCOTT

First name(s) **B3** EDWARD JOHN

Date of birth **B4** 2 / 2 / 1947   Date of death **B5** 27 / 7 / 2003

Marital status **B6** MARRIED   Last known usual address

Surviving relatives   **B7** 16 JAMES COURT
                                       BATH

Husband/Wife **B8** ✓

Brother(s)/Sister(s) **B9** ✓

Parent(s) **B10** ✓   Postcode BA7 4NH

Number of   Nursing / Residential home **B13**

Children **B11** 2   Domicile **B14** ENGLAND AND WALES

Grandchildren **B12**   Occupation **B15** SALES MANAGER

National Insurance number **B16** X Y 1 2 3 4 5 6 A

Income tax district **B17** BRISTOL 1

Income tax reference or self assessment reference **B18** 12345 67890

C **Solicitor or other person to contact**

Name and address of firm or person
dealing with the estate

C1 MELANIE SCOTT   Telephone number
     17 ARUNDEL WAY   **C4** 0117 123456
     BRISTOL
                             Fax number
                             C5

     Postcode BS8 3JQ

DX number and town   For CTO use

C2

Contact name and reference

C3 MISS M. SCOTT   **IHT 200**

R2H4114CTO11/99

D Supplementary pages

You must answer all of the questions in this section. You should read the notes starting at page 10 of form IHT 210 before answering the questions.

If you answer "Yes" to a question you will need to fill in the supplementary page shown. If you do not have all the supplementary pages you need you should telephone our Orderline on 0845 2341000.

		No	Yes	Page
● **The Will**	Did the deceased leave a Will?		✓	D1
● **Domicile outside the United Kingdom**	Was the deceased domiciled outside the UK at the date of death?	✓		D2
● **Gifts and other transfers of value**	Did the deceased make any gift or any other transfer of value on or after 18 March 1986?		✓	D3
● **Joint assets**	Did the deceased hold any asset(s) in joint names with another person?		✓	D4
● **Nominated assets**	Did the deceased, at any time during their lifetime, give written instructions (usually called a "nomination") that any asset was to pass to a particular person on their death?	✓		D4
● **Assets held in trust**	Did the deceased have any right to any benefit from any assets held in trust or in a settlement at the date of death?	✓		D5
● **Pensions**	Did the deceased have provision for a pension, other than the State Pension, from employers, a personal pension policy or other provisions made for retirement?	✓		D6
● **Stocks and shares**	Did the deceased own any stocks or shares?		✓	D7
● **Debts due to the estate**	Did the deceased lend any money, either on mortgage or by personal loan, that had not been repaid by the date of death?	✓		D8
● **Life insurance and annuities**	Did the deceased pay any premiums on any life insurance policies or annuities which are payable to either the estate or to someone else or which continue after death?		✓	D9
● **Household and personal goods**	Did the deceased own any household goods or other personal possessions?		✓	D10
● **Interest in another estate**	Did the deceased have a right to a legacy or a share of an estate of someone who died before them, but which they had not received before they died?	✓		D11
● **Land, buildings and interests in land**	Did the deceased own any land or buildings in the UK?		✓	D12
● **Agricultural relief**	Are you deducting agricultural relief?	✓		D13
● **Business interests**	Did the deceased own all or part of a business or were they a partner in a business?	✓		D14
● **Business relief**	Are you deducting business relief?	✓		D14
● **Foreign assets**	Did the deceased own any assets outside the UK?	✓		D15
● **Debts owed by the estate**	Are you claiming a deduction against the estate for any money that the deceased had borrowed from relatives, close friends, or trustees, or other loans, overdrafts or guarantee debts?	✓		D16

2

E **Domicile in Scotland**

- Has any claim for legal rights been made or discharged?   No ☐ Yes ☐

- How many children are under 18 ☐ or 18 and over ☐

F **Estate in the UK where tax may not be paid by instalments**

• Quoted stocks, shares and investments *(box SS1, form D7)*	**F1** £46,396
• UK Government and municipal securities *(box SS2, form D7)*	**F2** £2,500
• Unquoted stocks, shares and investments	**F3** £3,750
• Traded unquoted stocks and shares	**F4** £
• Dividends or interest	**F5** £374
• Premium Bonds	**F6** £300
• National Savings investments *(show details on form D17)*	**F7** £
• Bank and building society accounts *(show details on form D17)*	**F8** £34,374
• Cash	**F9** £50
• Debts due to the deceased and secured by mortgage *(box DD1, form D8)*	**F10** £
• Other debts due to the deceased *(box DD1, form D8)*	**F11** £
• Rents due to the deceased	**F12** £
• Accrued income	**F13** £
• Apportioned income	**F14** £
• Other income due to the deceased *(box IP4, form D9, box PA1 form D6)*	**F15** £88
• Life insurance policies *(box IP3, form D9)*	**F16** £10,650
• Private health schemes	**F17** £
• Income tax or capital gains tax repayment	**F18** £
• Household and personal goods *(sold, box HG1, form D10)*	**F19** £
• Household and personal goods *(unsold, box HG2, form D10)*	**F20** £25,600
• Interest in another estate *(box UE1, form D11)*	**F21** £
• Interest in expectancy *(reversionary interest)*	**F22** £
• Other personal assets in the UK *(show details on form D17)*	**F23** £148
Total assets *(sum of boxes F1 to F23)*	**F24** £124,230

3

Liabilities, funeral expenses, exemptions and reliefs

- Liabilities

Name	Description of liability	
BARCLAYCARD	OUTSTANDING CREDIT CARD BALANCE	239
BRITISH TELECOM	BILL TO DATE OF DEATH	52
F JARVIS	PLUMBING SERVICES	46

Total liabilities **F25** £337

- Funeral expenses

1,275

Total of funeral expenses **F26** £ 1,275

Total liabilities and funeral expenses *(box F25 plus box F26)* **F27** £ 1,612

Net total of assets less liabilities *(box F24 less box F27)* **F28** £122,618

- Exemptions and reliefs

Total exemptions and reliefs **F29** £NIL

Chargeable value of assets in the UK where tax may not be paid by instalments *(box F28 less box F29)* **F30** £122,618

4

G **Estate in the UK where tax may be paid by instalments**

Do you wish to pay the tax on these assets by instalments?   No ☐   Yes ✓

- Deceased's residence — **G1** £ 165,000
- Other residential property — **G2** £
- Farms — **G3** £
- Business property — **G4** £
- Timber and woodland — **G5** £
- Other land and buildings — **G6** £

- Farming business — Interest in a business **G7.1** £ — Interest in a partnership **G7.2** £ — **G7** £
- Other business interests — Interest in a business **G8.1** £ — Interest in a partnership **G8.2** £ — **G8** £
- Business assets — Farm trade assets **G9.1** £ — Other business assets **G9.2** £ — **G9** £

- Quoted shares and securities, control holding only — **G10** £

- Unquoted shares — Control holding **G11.1** £ — Non-control holding **G11.2** £ — **G11** £
- Traded unquoted shares — Control holding **G12.1** £ — Non-control holding **G12.2** £ — **G12** £

Total assets *(sum of boxes G1 to G12)* **G13** £ 165,000

Liabilities, exemptions and reliefs

- Name and address of mortgagee

  HALIFAX PLC, BATH BRANCH ON 16 JAMES COURT, BATH

  G14 £ 17,052

- Other liabilities

  Total of other liabilities **G15** £

  Net total of assets less liabilities *(box G13 less boxes G14 and G15)* **G16** £ 147,948

- Exemptions and reliefs

  Total exemptions and reliefs **G17** £

  Chargeable value of assets in the UK where tax may be paid by instalments *(box G16 less box G17)* **G18** £ 147,948

5

H Summary of the chargeable estate

You should fill in form IHT(WS) so that you can copy the figures to this section and to section J.
If you are applying for a grant without the help of a solicitor or other agent and you do not wish to work out the tax yourself, leave this section and section J blank. Go on to section K.

Calculating the total tax that is payable

- Estate in the UK *(box WS1)* — **H1** £
- Joint property *(box WS2)* — **H2** £
- Foreign property *(box WS3)* — **H3** £
- Settled property on which the trustees would like to pay tax now *(box WS4)* — **H4** £

Total of assets where tax may not be paid by instalments *(box WS5)* **H5** £

Assets where tax may be paid by instalments

- Estate in the UK *(box WS6)* — **H6** £
- Joint property *(box WS7)* — **H7** £
- Foreign property *(box WS8)* — **H8** £
- Settled property on which the trustees would like to pay tax now *(box WS9)* — **H9** £

Total of assets where tax may not be paid by instalments *(box WS10)* **H10** £

Other property taken into account to calculate the total tax

- Settled property *(box WS11)* — **H11** £
- Gift with reservation *(box WS12)* — **H12** £

Chargeable estate *(box WS13)* **H13** £

Cumulative total of lifetime transfers *(box WS14)* **H14** £

Aggregate chargeable transfer *(box WS15)* **H15** £

Note: In this example, these sections of the form have been left blank, as the executors of Edward John Scott's estate wish the Capital Taxes Office to calculate the inheritance tax.

J Calculating the tax liability

Calculating the total tax that is payable

- Aggregate chargeable transfer *(box WS16)* **J1** £
- Tax threshold *(box WS17)* **J2** £
- Value chargeable to tax *(box WS18)* **J3** £

  Tax payable *(box WS19)* **J4** £

- Tax (if any) payable on lifetime transfers *(box WS20)* **J5** £
- Relief for successive charges *(box WS21)* **J6** £

  Tax payable on total of assets liable to tax *(box WS22)* **J7** £

Calculating the tax payable on delivery of this account

- Tax which may not be paid by instalments *(box TX4)* **J8** £
- Double taxation relief *(box TX5)* **J9** £
- Interest to be added *(box TX7)* **J10** £

  Tax and interest being paid now which may not be paid by instalments *(box TX8)* **J11** £

- Tax which may be paid by instalments *(box TX12)* **J12** £
- Double taxation relief *(box TX13)* **J13** £
- Number of instalments being paid now **J14** / 10 *(box TX15)*
- Tax now payable *(box TX16)* **J15** £
- Interest on instalments to be added *(box TX17)* **J16** £
- Additional interest to be added *(box TX18)* **J17** £

Tax and interest being paid now which may be paid by instalments *(box TX19)* **J18** £

Total tax and interest being paid now on this account *(box TX20)* **J19** £

K Authority for repayment of inheritance tax

In the event of any inheritance tax being overpaid the payable order for overpaid tax and interest in connection with this estate should be made out to

MELANIE SCOTT, 17 ARUNDEL WAY, BRISTOL B38 3JQ

7

Declaration

I/We wish to apply for a | **L1** | GRANT OF PROBATE OF THE WILL

To the best of my/our knowledge and belief, the information *I*/we have given and the statements *I*/we have made in this account and in supplementary pages | **L2** | D1, D3, D4, D7, D9, D10, D12 attached (together called "this account") are correct and complete.

I/We have made the fullest enquiries that are reasonably practicable in the circumstances to find out the opern market value of all the items shown in this account. The value of items in box(es)

| **L3** | | are provisional

estimates which are based on all the information available to me/us at this time. *I*/We will tell Capital Taxes Office the exact value(s) as soon as *I*/we know it and *I*/we will pay any additional tax and interest that may be due.

I/We understand that *I*/we may be liable to prosecution if *I*/we deliberately conceal any information that affects the liability to inheritance tax arising on the deceased's death, OR if *I*/we deliberately include information in this account which *I*/we know to be false.

I/We understand that *I*/we may have to pay financial penalties if this account is incorrect by reason of my/our fraud or negligence, OR if *I*/we fail to remedy anything in this account which is incorrect in any material respect within a reasonable time of it coming to my/our notice.

I/We understand that the issue of the grant does not mean that

- I/we have paid all the inheritance tax and interest that may be due on the estate, or

- the statements made and the vlaues included in this account are accepted by Capital Taxes Office.

I/We understand that Capital Taxes Office

- will only look at this account in detail after the grant has been issued

- may need to ask further questions and discuss the value of items shown in this account

- may make further calculations of tax and interest payable to help the persons liable for the tax make provision to meet the tax liability.

I/We understand that where we have elected to pay tax by instalments that *I*/we may have to pay interest on any unpaid tax according to the law.

Each person delivering this account, whether as executor, intending administrator or otherwise must sign below to indicate that they have read and agreed the statements above.

Full name and address	*Full name and address*
MELANIE SCOTT 17 ARUNDEL WAY BRISTOL BS8 3JQ	ROSEMARY JANE RAYNER 98 CHURCHILL ROAD SWINDON SN9 4SZ
Signature Melanie Scott *Date* 1/8/03	*Signature* R Rayner *Date* 1/8/03
Full name and address	*Full name and address*
Signature *Date*	*Signature* *Date*

8

Inland **Revenue**
Capital Taxes Office

The Will

Name

EDWARD JOHN SCOTT

Date of death

27 / 7 / 2003

Give details about the latest Will made by the deceased. If a Deed of Variation has been signed before applying for a grant, fill in the form to show the effect of the Will and the Deed together. You should read form D1(Notes) before filling in this form.

1 Is the address for the deceased as shown in the Will the same as the address on page 1 of form IHT200?

No ☐ Yes ✓

If the answer is "No", say below what happened to the property shown in the Will.

2 Are all items referred to in the Will, for example, legacies referring to personal possessions, stocks and shares, loans or gifts made by the deceased, included in form IHT200?

N/A ☐ No ☐ Yes ✓

If the answer is "No", say below why these items are not included.

3 Does the whole estate pass to beneficiaries who are chargeable to inheritance tax?

No ✓ Yes ☐

If the answer is "No", deduct the exemption on form IHT200.

D1

R0G4113

Reproduced by Law Pack Publishing with the permission of the Controller of HMSO

Continuation sheet for additional information

Inland **Revenue**
Capital Taxes Office

Name	Date of death
EDWARD JOHN SCOTT	27 / 7 / 2003

Use this form as a continuation sheet or to give any additional information that we ask for. Show the box number on form IHT200 or the supplementary page number the information relates to. You should read form D17(Notes) before filling in this form.

Box or page number	Additional information	£
F8	**BANK AND BUILDING SOCIETY ACCOUNTS**	
	BRISTOL CITY BUILDING SOCIETY	
	ACCOUNT No: 1234568	
	BALANCE AT DEATH 12,000.00	
	INTEREST ACCRUED TO DEATH 196.00	12,196.00
	BARCLAYS BANK PLC	
	DEPOSIT ACCOUNT No: 345821	
	BALANCE AT DEATH 15,626.00	
	INTEREST ACCRUED TO DEATH 300.00	15,926.00
	HALIFAX PLC	
	LIQUID GOLD ACCOUNT No: 342816	
	BALANCE AT DEATH 6,100.00	
	INTEREST ACCRUED TO DEATH 152.00	6,252.00
F23	**REFUND OF BUPA SUBSCRIPTION**	148.00

D17

Reproduced by Law Pack Publishing with the permission of the Controller of HMSO

Please turn over

R0H4171

Inland Revenue
Capital Taxes Office

Probate summary

Fill in this page to give details of the estate that becomes the property of the personal representatives of the deceased. It is this property for which the grant of representation is to be made. You should read form D18(Notes) before filling in this form.

A Name and address

MELANIE SCOTT
17 ARUNDEL WAY
BRISTOL
BS8 3JQ

Probate registry

BRISTOL

Date of grant
(for probate registry use)

B About the person who has died

| Title | MR | Surname | SCOTT |

First name(s) EDWARD JOHN

Date of death 27 / 7 /2003

Domicile ENGLAND AND WALES

Last known usual address

16 ST JAMES COURT
BATH

Postcode BA7 4NH

C **Summary from IHT200**
Add the value of any general power
property on form D5 to boxes PS1–PS5

Gross assets, section F, box 24	**PS1**	£ 124,230
Gross assets, section G, box 13	**PS2**	£ 165,000
Gross value to be carried to Probate papers *(box PS1 plus box PS2)*	**PS3**	£ 289,230
Liabilities, section F, box F27	**PS4**	£ 1,612
Liabilities, section G, boxes G14 plus G15	**PS5**	£ 17,052
Net value to be carried to Probate papers *(box PS3 less box PS4 less box PS5)*	**PS6**	£ 270,566
Total value for life insurance policies, section J, box J19	**PS7**	£

Signature of person or firm calculating the amount due   Contact name and/or reference   Date   / /

(For CTO use only)

CTO reference

EDP

Cashier's reference

CTO Cashiers

D18

Reproduced by Law Pack Publishing with the permission of the Controller of HMSO

R0G4109

Gifts and other transfers of value

Inland Revenue
Capital Taxes Office

Name	Date of death
EDWARD JOHN SCOTT	27 / 7 / 2003

You have said that the deceased had transferred assets during their lifetime. Answer the following questions and give the further details we ask for. You should read form D3(Notes) before filling in this form.

1 Did the deceased within seven years of their death

1a make any gift or transfer to, or for the benefit of, another person? — No ☐ Yes ✓

1b create any trust or settlement? — No ✓ Yes ☐

1c pay any premium on a life insurance policy for the benefit of someone else other than the deceased's spouse? *(see also form D9, question 5)* — No ✓ Yes ☐

1d cease to have any right to benefit from any assets held in trust or in a settlement? — No ✓ Yes ☐

If the answer to any part of question 1 is "Yes", fill in the details we ask for below

Date of gift	Name and relationship of recipient and description of assets	Value at date of gift	Amount and type of exemption claimed	Net value after exemptions
15TH OCT 1998	JAMES PETER SCOTT 73 JAMES STREET LONDON SE1 4XX (FATHER) CASH	£5,000		
	LESS: ANNUAL EXEMPTION FOR 1998/99 AND 1997/98		£6,000	NIL

		Total LT1 £ NIL

Please turn over

D3

R0H4164

Gifts with reservation

2 Did the deceased transfer any assets during their lifetime but

2a the person receiving the gift did not take full possession of it, or   No ✓   Yes

2b the deceased continued to have some right to benefit from all or part of the asset?   No ✓   Yes

If the answer to any part of question 2 is "Yes", fill in the details we ask for below

Date of gift	Name and relationship of recipient and description of assets	Value at date of gift	Amount and type of exemption claimed	Net value after exemptions

Total **LT2** £

Earlier transfers

3 Did the deceased make any *chargeable* transfers during the 7 years before the earliest date of the gifts shown at boxes LT1 and LT2 above?   No ✓   Yes

If the answer to question 3 is "Yes", fill in the details below, but do not include the value in any of the tax calculations.

Date of gift	Name and relationship of recipient and description of assets	Value at date of gift	Amount and type of exemption claimed	Net value after exemptions

Joint and nominated assets

Inland Revenue
Capital Taxes Office

Name	Date of death
EDWARD JOHN SCOTT	27 / 7 / 2003

Give details of any assets that the deceased owned jointly with another person or people. If necessary use a separate form for each item. Give details of any property that the deceased had nominated during their lifetime. You should read from D4(Notes) before filling in this form.

1 Bank and building society accounts, stocks, shares, unit trusts, household effects etc

If the value of the deceased's share is **not** the **whole** value, say

- who the other joint owner(s) is or are — JULIA ANNE SCOTT (WIDOW)
- when the joint ownership began — ACCOUNT OPENED 2/2/91
- how much each joint owner provided to obtain the item — HALF EACH
- who received the income or interest, if there was any — HALF EACH
- who received the benefit of any withdrawals from bank or building society accounts, if any were made — HALF EACH
- whether the item passes to other joint owner(s) by survivorship or under the deceased's Will or intestacy. — JOINT OWNERSHIP BY SURVIVORSHIP

Details of each item	Whole value	Deceased's share
BARCLAYS BANK CURRENT ACCOUNT	3,746	1,873

- Liabilities

	Total of assets	JP1	£ 1,873
	Total of liabilities.	JP2	£
	Net assets *(box JP1 less box JP2)*	JP3	£ 1,873

- Exemptions and reliefs

SURVIVING SPOUSE	1,873

Total exemptions and reliefs	JP4	£ 1,873

Net total of joint assets passing by survivorship where tax may not be paid by instalments *(box JP3 less box JP4)*	JP5	£ NIL

Please turn over

D4

Reproduced by Law Pack Publishing with the permission of the Controller of HMSO

R0H4165

2 **Land, buildings, business assets, control shareholdings and unquoted shares**

Do you wish to pay tax on these assets by instalments? **No** **Yes**

If the value of the deceased's share is **not** the **whole** value, say

- who the other joint owner(s) is or are
- when the joint ownership began
- how much each joint owner provided to obtain the item
- who received the income or interest, if there was any
- whether the item passes to other joint owner(s) by survivorship or under the deceased's Will or intestacy.

Details of each item	Whole value	Deceased's share

- Liabilities

Total of assets **JP6** £

Total of liabilities **JP7** £

- Exemptions and reliefs

Net assets *(box JP6 less box JP7)* **JP8** £

Total exemptions and reliefs **JP9** £

Net total of joint assets passing by survivorship where tax may be paid by instalments *(box JP8 less box JP9)* **JP10** £

3 **Nominated property**

If the deceased nominated any assets to any person, describe the assets below, and show their value.

Include the assets in the appropriate box in section F of form IHT200.

Inland Revenue
Capital Taxes Office

Stocks and shares

Name

EDWARD JOHN SCOTT

Date of death

27 / 7 / 2003

Give details about the stocks and shares included in the deceased's estate. You should read form D7(Notes) before filling in this form.

1 **Quoted stocks, shares and investments** *(see box 2 for government securities)*

Name of company and type of shares or stock, or **full** name of unit trust and type of units	Number of shares or units or amount of stock held	Market price at date of death	Total value at date of death	Dividend or interest due to date of death	For CTO use only
Quoted on Stock Exchange					
BAT INDUSTRIES ORDINARY 25p SHARES	1,106	5.3375XD	5,903.27	102.30	
GLAXOSMITHKLINE ORDINARY 25p SHARES	1,000	7.89XD	7,890.00	200.00	
MARKS & SPENCER ORDINARY 25p SHARES	1,200	4.3625	5,235.00		
UNILEVER ORDINARY 25p SHARES	2,200	12.44	27,368.00		
		Total(s) SS1	£46,396.27	£ 302.30	

Copy the total from box SS1 to box F1, page 3, form IHT200.
Include the total of all dividends and interest in box FS, page 3.

D7

Please turn over

R0H4167

2 UK Government and municipal securities

Description of stock	Amount of stock £	Market price at date of death	Total value at date of death	Interest due to date of death	For CTO use only
TREASURY 8% STOCK 2003	2,500	100.00	2,500.00	71.78	

Total(s) **SS2** £ 2,500.00 | £ 71.78

Copy the total from box SS2 to box F2, page 3, form IHT200.
Include the total of all dividends and interest in box F5, page 3.

3 Unquoted stocks, shares and investments

Name of company and type of share or stock	Number of shares	Price per share	Total value of shares	Dividend due to date of death	For CTO use only
XYZ ELECTRONICS LIMITED (Registered number 1234567) Ordinary shares	2,500	1.50	3,750.00		

Include the value of the shares in box F3, page 3 or box G11, page 5, form IHT200.
Include the total of all dividends in box F5, page 3.

4 Traded unquoted stocks and shares

Name of company and type of share or stock	Number of shares	Price per share	Total value of shares	Dividend due to date of death	For CTO use only

Include the value of the shares in box F4, page 3 or box G12, page 5, form IHT200.
Include the total of all dividends in box F5, page 3.

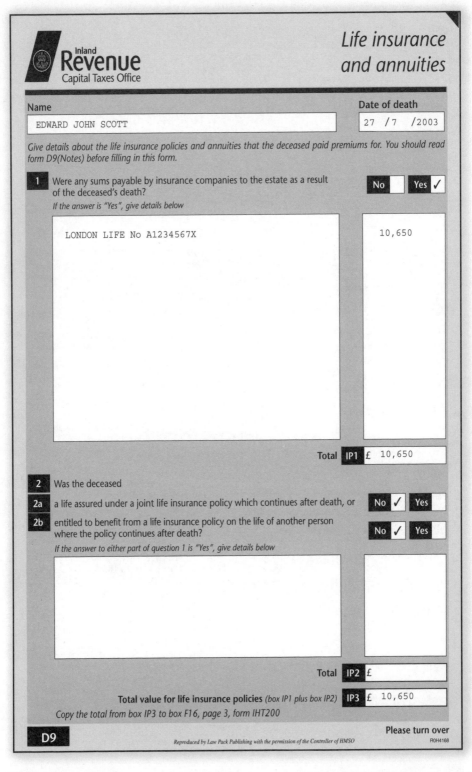

3 Did any payments made under a purchased life annuity continue after the deceased's death?

No ✓   Yes

If the answer is "Yes", give details below

Total **IP4** £

Include the total from box IP4 in box F15, page 3, form IHT200.

4 Was a lump sum payable under a purchased life annuity as a result of the deceased's death?

No ✓   Yes

If the answer is "Yes", give details below

Total **IP5** £

Include the total from box IP5 in box F23, page 3, form IHT200.

5 Did the deceased, within 7 years of their death, pay any premium on a life insurance policy for the benefit of someone else, other than the deceased's spouse?

No ✓   Yes

6 Did the deceased have some right to benefit from a life insurance policy taken out on another person's life and held in trust for the benefit of the deceased (and others)?

No ✓   Yes

If the answer to either questions 5 or 6 is "Yes", you should read form D9(Notes) to find out what you should do.

Household and personal goods

Inland **Revenue**
Capital Taxes Office

Name	Date of death
EDWARD JOHN SCOTT	27 / 7 / 2003

Give details about the life household goods or other personal property owned by the deceased. You should read form D10(Notes) before filling in this form..

1 If any household goods and other personal possessions have **already been sold**, fill in the **gross** sale proceeds below.

Gross proceeds of sale **HG1** £

Copy the value from box HG1 to box F19, page 3, form IHT200.

2 If you have obtained any valuation(s) of the household goods and other personal possessions that have not been sold, enter the total figure in the box below.

If no valuation has been obtained, give brief details of the items and their value.

See valuation of Phillips, valuers, attached	25,600

Total value of household and personal goods unsold **HG2** £ 25,600

Copy the value from box HG2 to box F20, page 3, form IHT200.

3 Are any of the unsold items going to be sold?   Unknown ✓   No   Yes

4 Say below how the value for the unsold items has been established. If you have given a low total value, or the value is "Nil", say why this is so.

D10

Reproduced by Law Pack Publishing with the permission of the Controller of HMSO   R0J4120

Land, buildings and interests in land

Inland Revenue
Capital Taxes Office

Name

EDWARD JOHN SCOTT

Date of death

27 / 7 / 2003

CTO reference

Give the details we ask for about the land included in the deceased's estate. You should read form D12(Notes) before filling in this form.

1 Name and address of the person that the Valuation Office should contact

Reference

MELANIE SCOTT
17 ARUNDEL WAY
BRISTOL BS8 3JQ

Telephone number

0117 123456

2

A Item No.	B Full address (including postcode) or description of property	C Tenure	D Lettings/leases	E Agricultural, timber or heritage element	F Open market value
1	16 JAMES COURT, BATH BA7 4NH	FREEHOLD	NONE	NONE	165,000
			Total(s) carried forward	£	165,000

Please turn over
R0H4169

Reproduced by Law Pack Publishing with the permission of the Controller of HMSO

D12

233

Land, buildings and interests in land

Inland Revenue — Capital Taxes Office

Name

MICHAEL STEPHEN BROWN

CTO reference

Date of death

15 / 6 / 2003

Give the details we ask for about the land included in the deceased's estate. You should read form D12(Notes) before filling in this form.

Name and address of the person that the Valuation Office should contact

Reference

MRS FRANCES BROWN
17 PETER STREET
IPSWICH IP15 2JH

Telephone number

0117 123456

A Item No.	B Full address (including postcode) or description of property	C Tenure	D Lettings/leases	E Agricultural, timber or heritage element	F Open market value
1	17 PETER STREET IPSWICH IP15 2JH (Deceased's half share)	FREEHOLD	NONE	NONE	60,000
			Total(s) carried forward	£	£ 60,000

Please turn over
R0H4169

Reproduced by Law Pack Publishing with the permission of the Controller of HMSO

D12

234

STOCK TRANSFER FORM			
		(Above this line for Registrars only)	

Certificate lodged with the Registrar

Consideration Money £ NIL

(For completion by the Registrar/Stock Exchange)

Name of Undertaking	LAW PACK PUBLISHING LIMITED
Description of Security	ORDINARY 25P SHARES

Number or amount of Shares, Stock or other security and, in figures column only, number and denomination of units, if any.	Words SIX HUNDRED	Figures (600 units of 25P)

Names(s) of registered holder(s) should be given in full: the address should be given where there is only one holder. If the transfer is not made by the registered holder(s) insert also the name(s) and capacity (e.g. Executor(s) of the person(s) making the transfer).	In the name(s) of **EDWARD JOHN SCOTT OF 16 JAMES COURT, BATH, BA7 4NH BY HIS PERSONAL REPRESENTATIVES, MELANIE SCOTT AND ROSEMARY JANE RAYNER**

I/We hereby transfer the above security out of the name(s) aforesaid to the person(s) named below.

Signature(s) of transferor(s)

1. *Melanie Scott*
2. *R Rayner*
3.
4.

A body corporate should execute this transfer under its common seal or otherwise in accordance with applicable statutory requirements.

Stamp of Selling Broker(s) or, for transactions which are not stock exchange transactions, of Agent(s), if any, acting for the Transferor(s)

Date   10TH DECEMBER 2003

Full name(s) and full postal address(es) (including County or, if applicable, Postal District number) of the person(s) to whom the security is transferred. Please state title, if any, or whether Mr., Mrs. or Miss. Please complete in typewriting or Block Capitals.	MRS ROSEMARY JANE RAYNER 98 CHURCHILL ROAD SWINDON SN9 4SZ

I/We request that such entries be made in the register as are necessary to give effect to this transfer.

Stamp of Buying Broker(s) (if any)	Stamp or name and address of person lodging this form (if other than the Buying Broker(s))
	MELANIE SCOTT 17 ARUNDEL WAY BRISTOL BS8 3JQ

Reference to the Registrar in this Form means the registrar or registration agent of the undertaking NOT the Registrar of Companies at Companies House.

Form of certificate required where transfer is exempt from stamp duty

Instruments of transfer executed on or after 1st May 1987 are exempt from stamp duty if the transaction falls within any of the following categories:

A. The vesting of property subject to a trust in the trustees of the trust on the appointment of a new trustee, or in the continuing trustees on the retirement of a trustee.

B. The conveyance or transfer of property the subject of a specific devise or legacy to the beneficiary named in the will (or his nominee). Transfers in satisfaction of a general legacy of money should not be included in this category (see category D below).

C. The conveyance or transfer of property which forms part of an intestate's estate to the person entitled on intestacy (or his nominee). Transfers in satisfaction of the transferees entitlement to cash in the estate of an intestate, where the total value of the residuary estate exceeds that sum, should not be included in this category (see category D below).

D. The appropriation of property within section 84(4) of the Finance Act 1985 (death: appropriation in satisfaction of a general legacy of money) or section 84(5) or (7) of that Act (death: appropriation in satisfaction of any interest of surviving spouse and in Scotland also of any interest of issue).

E. The conveyance or transfer of property which forms part of the residuary estate of a testator to a beneficiary (or his nominee) entitled solely by virtue of his entitlement under the will.

F. The conveyance or transfer of property out of a settlement in or towards satisfaction of a beneficiary's interest, not being an interest acquired for money or money's worth, being a conveyance or transfer constituting a distribution of property in accordance with the provisions of the settlement.

G. The conveyance or transfer of property on and in consideration only of marriage to a party to the marriage (or his nominee) or to trustees to be held on the terms of a settlement made in consideration only of the marriage. A transfer to a spouse after the date of marriage is not within this category, unless made pursuant to an ante-nuptial contract.

H. The conveyance or transfer of property within section 83(1) of the Finance Act 1985 (transfers in connection with divorce etc.).

I. The conveyance or transfer by the liquidator of property which formed part of the assets of the company in liquidation to a shareholder of that company (or his nominee) in or towards satisfaction of the shareholder's rights on a winding-up.

J. The conveyance or transfer of property operating as a voluntary disposition *inter vivos* for no consideration in money or money's worth nor any consideration referred to in section 57 of the Stamp Act 1891 (conveyance in consideration of a debt etc.).

K. The conveyance or transfer of property by an instrument within section 84(1) of the Finance Act 1985 (death: varying disposition).

* Delete as appropriate.

*I/We hereby certify that the transaction in respect of which this transfer is made is one which falls within category E above.

*I/We confirm that *I/we have been authorised by the transferor to sign this certificate and that the facts of the transaction are within *my/our knowledge.

Signature(s)

Melanie Scott   Description or capacity ('Transferor', 'Solicitor', etc.)
                          EXECUTOR

R Rayner   EXECUTOR

Date   12/12/   20 03

Notes:
(1) If the above certificate has been completed, this transfer does not need to be submitted to an Inland Revenue Stamp Office.
(2) If the above certificate has not been completed, this transfer needs to be submitted to an Inland Revenue Stamp Office and duly stamped.

Form of certificate required where transfer is not liable to *ad valorem* stamp duty

Some instruments of transfer are liable to a fixed duty of £5.00 when the transaction falls within one of the following categories:

(a) Transfer by way of security for a loan or re-transfer to the original transferor on repayment of a loan.

(b) Transfer, not on sale and not arising under any contract of sale and where no beneficial interest in the property passes: (i) to a person who is a mere nominee of, and is nominated only by, the transferor; (ii) from a mere nominee who has at all times held the property on behalf of the transferee; (iii) from one nominee to another nominee of the same beneficial owner where the first nominee has at all times held the property on behalf of that beneficial owner. (NOTE - This category does not include a transfer made in any of the following circumstances: (i) by a holder of stock, etc., following the grant of an option to purchase the stock, to the person entitled to the option or his nominee; (ii) to a nominee in contemplation of a contract for the sale of the stock, etc., then about to be entered into; (iii) from the nominee of a vendor, who has instructed the nominee orally or by some unstamped writing to hold stock, etc., in trust for a purchaser, to such purchaser.)

* Delete as appropriate.

*I/We hereby certify that the transaction in respect of which this transfer is made is one which falls within the category _____ above.

*I/We confirm that *I/we have been duly authorised by the transferor to sign this certificate and that the facts of the transaction are within *my/our knowledge.

Signature(s)   Description or capacity ('Transferor', 'Solicitor', etc.)

Date _____ 20 _____

Index

The index covers the main text, but not the appendices. Entries categorise Wills, Power of Attorney and probate, the principal subjects of the book.

MORE BOOKS AVAILABLE FROM LAWPACK

Employment Law Made Easy

Written by an employment law solicitor, *Employment Law Made Easy* is a comprehensive, reader-friendly source of information that will provide answers to practically all your employment law questions. Essential knowledge for employers and employees. Valid for use in England & Wales, and Scotland.

Code B702 | ISBN 1 904053 88 2 | Paperback | 153 x 234mm | 224pp | £11.99 | 6th edition

Health & Safety at Work Essentials

Every workplace has to comply with an extensive range of health and safety rules and regulations. With more legal claims being made daily, the price for failing to comply, whether through fines or claims by employees, can be high. This handy, 'one-stop' handbook sets out the background legal basics and provides succinct, practical advice on what measures to take.

Code B435 | ISBN 1 904053 77 7 | Paperback | 153 x 234mm | 176pp | £9.99 | 4th edition

Leaves on the Line!

Faulty goods, shoddy service, poor advice... these are things most of us, at some time, feel we have good reason to complain about. In this handbook, Steve Wiseman draws on his extensive experience as a Citizens Advice Bureau manager and tells you how to ensure your complaint has maximum impact, whether it be against your local shop or a government department.

Code B430 | ISBN 1 904053 67 X | Paperback | A5 | 208pp | £7.99 | 2nd edition

To order, visit **www.lawpack.co.uk** or call **020 7394 4040**

MORE BOOKS AVAILABLE FROM LAWPACK

Residential Lettings

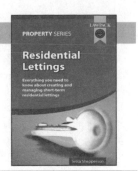

Are you thinking of letting a flat or a house? This guide steers anyone who intends – or already is – letting property through the legal and practical issues involved. It provides all the up-to-date information and tips that a would-be landlord needs. It will also alert existing landlords to the points of good practice that make a letting successful, and the legal obligations that they may not be aware of.

Code B622 | ISBN 1 904053 90 4 | Paperback | 153 x 234mm | 160pp | £11.99 | 5th edition

The Buy-to-Let Bible

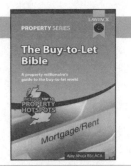

Low mortgage rates and under-performance by traditional savings and investment products means that property has never looked a better way to invest for the future. Author Ajay Ahuja divulges the practical and financial techniques that have made him a millionaire. It covers finding the right property, the right mortgage lender, the right tenant, legal issues and tax.

Code B637 | ISBN 1 904053 91 2 | Paperback | 153 x 234mm | 256pp | £11.99 | 3rd edition

The Seven Pillars of Buy-to-Let Wisdom

In his first, bestselling buy-to-let book, *The Buy-to-Let Bible* author and buy-to-let millionaire Ajay Ahuja provided the basics of successful buy-to-let. Ajay has now written 'further reading' for the buy-to-let investor, *The Seven Pillars of Buy-to-let Wisdom*, that explains in depth how to get the most from your investment by examining the seven fundamentals of successful buy-to-let property management.

Code B447 | ISBN 1 904053 42 4 | Paperback | 153 x 234mm | 144pp | £9.99 | 1st edition

To order, visit **www.lawpack.co.uk** or call **020 7394 4040**

MORE BOOKS AVAILABLE FROM LAWPACK

Book-Keeping Made Easy

This guide provides the new business owner with an understanding of the fundamental principles of book-keeping, showing how to set up accounts and how to benefit from the information they contain. Includes procedures for the sole proprietor and small business, accounting for growing businesses, double-entry book-keeping, ledgers, payroll and final accounts.

Code B516 | ISBN 1 904053 85 8 | Paperback | 153 x 234mm | 104pp | £10.99 | 2nd edition

Business Agreements Made Easy

This book's primary focus is business-to-business contracts for supply of services and/or goods with limited reference to business-to-consumer contracts. It explains the key commercial and legal issues which occur throughout a 'contract lifecycle' (i.e. from pre-contract stage to negotiation of contract to end of contract) with suggested actions and steps.

Code B519 | ISBN 1 904053 84 X | Paperback | 153 x 234mm | 144pp | £11.99 | 1st edition

Business Letters Made Easy

Business Letters Made Easy provides an invaluable source of 199 ready-drafted letters for a range of business situations. Each letter has a useful commentary, explaining when to use a particular letter and helping you choose the right turn of phrase. This book takes the headache and time-wasting out of letter writing, and provides you with letters that get results!

Code B520 | ISBN 1 904053 87 4 | Paperback | 153 x 234mm | 288pp | £12.99 | 1st edition

To order, visit **www.lawpack.co.uk** or call **020 7394 4040**

MORE BOOKS AVAILABLE FROM LAWPACK

101 Ways to Pay Less Tax

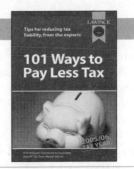

This book provides a wealth of tax saving tips from H M Williams Chartered Accountants, a national award winning firm of chartered accountants.

The tips included in this book are all legitimate ways to help reduce your tax bill – tax avoidance rather than tax evasion.

Code B448 | ISBN 1 904053 71 8 | Paperback | 153 x 234mm | 184pp | £9.99 | 1st edition

Proper Coffee

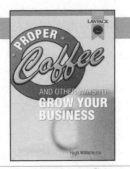

Management tomes abound but they can be turgid to wade through. This book provides a refreshing alternative for the small business. It provides succinct, practical advice on how to raise the bottom line and increase profitability, without working any harder.

Code B451 | ISBN 1 904053 86 6 | Paperback | 153 x 234mm | 150pp | £9.99 | 1st edition

Tax Answers at a Glance 2005/06

We all need to get to grips with the array of taxes now levied by the government. Compiled by award-winning tax experts and presented in question-and-answer format, this handbook provides a useful and digestible summary of Income Tax, Capital Gains Tax, Inheritance Tax, pensions, self-employment, partnerships, Corporation Tax, Stamp Duty/Land Tax, VAT, and more.

Code B625 | ISBN 1 904053 76 9 | Paperback | 153 x 234mm | 208pp | £9.99 | 5th edition

To order, visit **www.lawpack.co.uk** or call **020 7394 4040**

Visit the new Lawpack website and order online at www.lawpack.co.uk

What's new?

We've tried to retain the ease of use of our old site, while offering much more in terms of free legal information, more comprehensive product descriptions to give a true idea of what you're buying and links to qualified solicitors and legal resources if our products aren't appropriate for your situation.

Comprehensive product listings

First and foremost, Lawpack is a DIY legal publisher, and our ever-expanding range of easy-to-use titles is brought to life on the new website with extensive product overviews, author biographies, full content details and recommendations of other complementary titles in our range.

MORE BOOKS AVAILABLE FROM LAWPACK

301 Legal Forms, Letters & Agreements

Our best-selling form book is now in its eighth edition. It is packed with forms, letters and agreements for legal protection in many situations. It provides a complete do-it-yourself library of 301 ready-to-use legal documents, for business or personal use. Areas covered include loans and borrowing, buying and selling, employment, transfers and assignments and residential tenancy.

Code B402 | ISBN 1 904053 66 1 | Paperback | A4 | 384pp | £19.99 | 8th edition

Personnel Manager

A book of more than 200 do-it-yourself forms, contracts and letters to help your business manage its personnel records. Areas covered include recruitment and hiring, employment contracts and agreements, handling new employees, personnel management, performance evaluation and termination of employment.

Code B417 | ISBN 1 904053 23 8 | Paperback | A4 | 268pp | £14.99 | 3rd edition

Ready-Made Company Minutes & Resolutions

Maintaining good, up-to-date records of company meetings and resolutions is not only good practice but also a legal requirement, whatever size your company is. This book of forms makes compiling minutes of board and shareholder meetings straightforward. It includes more than 125 commonly-required resolutions and minutes to save you time and effort.

Code B616 | ISBN 1 904053 73 4 | Paperback | A4 | 192pp | £14.99 | 3rd edition

To order, visit **www.lawpack.co.uk** or call **020 7394 4040**